TOUCH
THE
FUTURE

"An absolutely pathbreaking collection of essays. . . . [John Lee] Clark places himself in an intellectual tradition of his forebearers, and finds meaning in the stylistic minutia of how one's identity is rendered on the page."

—Andrew Leland, *Millions*

"Deafblind poet Clark serves up passionate meditations on the Deafblind Protactile movement. . . . Clark's bracing perspectives are sure to stimulate. . . . Lucid and incisive, this is not to be missed." —*Publishers Weekly*, starred review

"In these compelling essays, Clark warmly welcomes us into this 'new world' [of Protactile], and his charm graces nearly every page. The author is a character in his own essays, weaving fables and legends together with undeniable craft. Funny, angry, and heroic, Clark is an amiable guide. . . . Throughout this lively journey, Clark . . . relishes his ability to tell tales, break rules, and possibly change the world. An epic and riotous book. Ignore it, and you might get left behind."

—*Kirkus Reviews*

"John Lee Clark writes against the grain with intellectual ferocity and dry wit; with linguistic playfulness and unsparing precision; and above all, with an expansive, curious, tireless compassion. Society may ignore and isolate DeafBlind people, but as Clark shows us again and again, it is the sighted and hearing world that is marginalized by its failure to understand DeafBlind life, and never the other way around."

—Andrew Leland, author of *The Country of the Blind: A Memoir at the End of Sight*

"John Lee Clark's fervent manifesto for the Protactile language and movement will blow your mind, enliven your body, and connect you to other people in unexpected ways. *Touch the Future* is a book that enlarges the human world."

—Edward Hirsch, author of *Stranger by Night: Poems*

"John Lee Clark's essays radiate with excitement and urgency. Tenderly documenting the emerging social movement of Protactile, they call upon us all to think about distance, power, and access in much bolder ways. To read Clark is not simply to be taught something by him, but to find yourself immersed and seeking alongside him—you don't just learn, you come away changed."   —Katie Booth, author of
The Invention of Miracles: Language, Power, and Alexander Graham Bell's Quest to End Deafness

"*Touch the Future* opens doors to the multiple worlds of disability. . . . This is a book for anyone who is interested in the life of the imagination and the mind."

—Stephen Kuusisto, author of *Eavesdropping: A Memoir of Blindness and Listening*

"John Lee Clark is equal parts master storyteller, wry comedian, erudite historian, and brilliant teacher. . . . At times urgent, often hilarious, and always illuminating, *Touch the*

Future will touch readers' hearts while opening their minds to a whole new world."

—Robert Sieburt, coauthor of *Deaf Utopia:
A Memoir—and a Love Letter to a Way of Life*

"Protactile leads the way in this exquisite book that invites us into the curious and joyful crafting of choreographies of encounter. . . . This is not a book to hold at a distance. This is a book that teaches us how to get into the tangle, knee against knee, hand enthusiastically tapping the thigh, to feel the world differently."

—Erin Manning, author of *For a Pragmatics of the Useless*

"Through John Lee Clark's writing, we witness the emergence of a new language, new sensibilities, new art forms, new forms of embodiment and sociality—nothing less than a new mode of existence. Clark's eloquent writing brings to voice one of the most significant cultural movements of our time."

—Brian Massumi, author of *Parables for the Virtual:
Movement, Affect, Sensation*

TOUCH
THE
FUTURE

TOUCH
THE
FUTURE

A MANIFESTO IN ESSAYS

John Lee Clark

W. W. NORTON & COMPANY

Independent Publishers Since 1923

For information about permission to reproduce selections from this book,
write to Permissions, W. W. Norton & Company, Inc.,
500 Fifth Avenue, New York, NY 10110

For information about special discounts for bulk purchases, please contact
W. W. Norton Special Sales at specialsales@wwnorton.com or 800-233-4830

Manufacturing by Lakeside Book Company
Book design by Brooke Koven
Production manager: Louise Mattarelliano

Library of Congress Control Number: 2024937836

ISBN 978–1-324–08641–3 pbk.

W. W. Norton & Company, Inc.
500 Fifth Avenue, New York, N.Y. 10110
www.wwnorton.com

W. W. Norton & Company Ltd.
15 Carlisle Street, London W1D 3BS

1 2 3 4 5 6 7 8 9 0

CONTENTS

x • *Contents*

PART FOUR • HOW IT FEELS TO US

TOUCH
THE
FUTURE

BY WAY OF
A DEDICATION

The spider's touch, how exquisitely fine!
Feels at each thread, and lives along the line . . .

—Alexander Pope, "An Essay on Man"

Welcome, welcome. Steady, friend. Here's a nice textured wall. I know, I know. You've stumbled into a new world. DeafBlind people have been here all along, but now everything is spinning faster than before. Everything you touch is alive with brave and precious pasts, which have now accrued and are opening up futures. This is the power of Protactile. We want to share it with you.

What is Protactile all about? It's hard to explain and easy to show. To say it's a movement DeafBlind people are leading isn't wrong. To say it's a new language enlisting tactile properties never used before in human communication is to state a fact. To say it's reinventing everything isn't hyperbole. The following pages will reveal the truth of these statements, but how to introduce such an epic event? It is said that an epic poem must open in the midst, in medias res. A revolution has many origins, too many threads to trace toward the center. Perhaps that's why the first book to emerge from the Protactile generation, the book you have in your hands, is a tangle of essays, any one of which can be the first to slide under your arm up to your hand and show you around.

And the exhilaration of this moment! Not a day passes without my whole body exclaiming: Yes! And: Why didn't we think of that before? And: I must tell everyone. A sense of jumping-up-and-down urgency overwhelms me. My joy, however, is tempered now and then by a pang, a lump in the throat. I think of my friends who have gone before me, who missed this moment, some of them dying just days before Protactile arrived. I like to think that deep down they knew. They were the beginnings, and my book is dedicated to them. Let me tell you about one of them.

I must have been eleven or twelve years old when our family friend Leslie Peterson came to stay with us in Minnesota. He had marital problems, the nature of which was kept a mystery to me, and he was shortly to move on to Seattle for a fruitful chapter of his life. He later returned to Minnesota, where I, now an adult, received him as a fellow tactile person and comrade in our local DeafBlind community. Back when my parents offered Leslie the use of our unfinished basement, my father was involved with Minnesota DeafBlind Association, but he hadn't yet gone tactile, as Leslie had. This meant that Leslie served as a role model for my father, me, and my younger brother. We all knew we would become quite blind like Leslie. We shared the same progressive-blindness condition that a certain percentage of Deaf people have called Usher syndrome. It is considered the leading etiology among

DeafBlind people and is hereditary, though as a recessive gene it usually leapfrogs multiple generations. I am one of the fortunate few to be second-generation DeafBlind.

Soon after his arrival and after my parents had shown him the hotel-style accommodations they had set up in the basement, I crept downstairs to watch Leslie. I found him pushing the pull-out sofa bed and rearranging the rug. He had moved the table. Then he stopped and turned toward me, reaching out with a hand. Fully expecting someone else's hand to slip underneath it.

Startled, I stepped back. Finding no hand to greet his, Leslie resumed his labors for a moment but stopped again. That's when I fled upstairs.

He would have known it hadn't been my father or mother who had been there. My mother, who is Deaf, and my father, a member of the DeafBlind community, would have automatically let Leslie know of their presence. My failure to render the courtesy remains one of my life regrets.

My sense of guilt notwithstanding, I loved hanging out with Leslie and doing chores with him. I soaked up countless details of DeafBlind ways. Talking with him filled me with what I later understood as intellectual pleasure. He was a born poet, a storyteller. His charisma was such that it cast a spell even when he wrote in English, a language in which he did not feel at home. Here is a passage from an email message he sent to our local community listserv many years later, recalling how he had first started to suspect that he had "eye problems":

> We lived in the wilderness or plain on the southeast corner of the Montana where my father was minister. We visited the large family of the farm. The young children of us went outdoor during the night with a strong light in the midst of

the farmland. We played touch and run. At the time I did not know that my vision were limited in the dark because I thought we all have the same ... I saw the shadow chase after me and I know she is coming to touch me. So I astray and ran from the shadow. I was surprised she ran faster than I. So I ran hardly zoom. She chased closer and closer to me. I hit the tractor so bad. I had bad injury and glasses broke. There is no doctor or hospital because we lived in the wilderness. My mother was the best doctor as the mother nature to cure my sores and new pair of glasses.

Leslie was ten times more compelling in American Sign Language. Every night during his stay, we eagerly gathered around him for a story. I believe it was that first night when he told us about the king and the spider.

Once upon a time, Leslie told us, there was a king at war. His armies had struggled and lost, struggled and lost, struggled and lost. So the king was pondering what to do. When the sun roused him from his troubled slumbers, he saw a web. He tore it down and sat to ponder.

The spider crawled up and swung here and there, building another web. When the king noticed this, he was annoyed and tore the new web down. He went back to resting his forehead on his fist. The spider swung here and there, once more building a web. The king was about to tear it down when he paused.

The king realized that the spider would never stop. He was inspired by its perseverance, and rallied his armies. They went to battle again, and this time victory was theirs.

Years later, I learned that this was the legend of Robert the Bruce, who was king of revolutionary and then independent Scotland from 1306 to 1329. After losing to the English in the Battle of Methven, Robert had become an outlaw, with his followers scattered and his wife held hostage. Some versions of the story have him hiding in a cave. Other versions have him in a hut. In the cave versions, the spider is trying to swing itself or throw a line to the opposite cave wall. In the hut versions, the spider is trying to connect with another beam of the roof. In some tellings, the spider makes this attempt two times before succeeding with the third, while most versions have it failing six times, with Robert the Bruce counting and remarking that he himself had lost to the English six times. If the spider failed a seventh time, Robert had decided, he would surrender to the English. If the spider succeeded, he would fight once more.

Leslie must have picked up the story and many others during his time at the Montana School for the Deaf and the Blind. It is easy to imagine how the story had morphed once it left the pages of an illustrated children's book, dancing away in the hands of ASL speakers. In no English version does the spider construct a web before the outlaw king observes it. It is always trying to make its first connection. There is never a web, to tear down or to leave be.

For many reasons, it is fitting that Leslie's version features extant webs being casually destroyed, only to have the spider weave another one. Leslie had spent much of his life as a Deaf-Blind person inexorably building a world, one unlike anything sanctioned by mainstream society. When I crept downstairs to watch Leslie get settled in, he was creating a particular kind of space. While he was able to maintain that space in our basement for the duration of his stay, his efforts elsewhere had been routinely and senselessly obliterated.

For as long as I knew him as an adult, Leslie wanted to work. "But," he told me, "I always fail." He explained how the pernicious local vocational rehabilitation agency would set up a new job goal and proceed to play the game of "job placement," where multiple hearing and sighted professionals got paid for helping Leslie secure a job that never materialized. This process was repeated many times over decades. Leslie made a little ditty out of the whole ordeal, which can be transliterated thus: "Goal, goal, goal, strive, strive, strive—fail! Goal, goal, goal, strive, strive, strive—fail!"

One of his talents was carpentry. His original creations vibrated with excellence. Tables, chairs, bureaus, chests. He also built, virtually single-handed, the garage adjacent to his house. Yet no factory or furniture manufacturer would hire him. On the factory floor, how would he know to stay within the yellow lines? In the furniture workshop, how would he read the penciled numbers on pre-cut pieces of wood? He had his ways of doing anything. The factories and workshops weren't interested in building a world with him; they preferred to keep the old one intact.

Leslie's efforts to find meaningful employment reached their nadir when he found himself doing light assembly at a workshop for mostly hearing and sighted disabled folks that paid below minimum wage. At least, he thought, he could just work, never mind the pay. At his work station, he developed his own logical, tactile world—just as he had in my parents' basement. When he picked up each fresh box of parts to assemble, he placed it on the counter, opened it, and worked with the parts with his arms still inside the box. He took only completed work out of the box. A lady came up to his counter and shook the parts out of the box onto a tray. Everyone else was using those trays. Leslie tried to explain that it was much easier to find the parts inside the box than to chase parts rolling around on the tray. He had it figured out and was completing pieces faster than anyone. Yet supervisors kept intervening and pouring the boxes' contents onto the tray. At last Leslie gathered his things, put on his coat, took up his white cane, and left.

After this experience, Leslie sent a quietly seething piece of formal writing to our community email group. "Who Is Disabled?" is an outstanding example of Protactile thought before the movement had even begun. Leslie's profound challenge is worth quoting in its entirety:

> HE looks at HER.
> HE learns SHE is the DeafBlind.
> HIS mind SHE is the disabled.
>
> Really? Which is the disabled person?
> HE or SHE?
>
> Yes, SHE is disabled.
> SHE can not hear any voice.
> SHE can not read any text messages.
> But HE is disabled, too.
>
> You might say, "No!"
> Because HE is the hearing-sighted.
> Of course, HE is DISABLED, too.
> HE can not talk to HER.
> HE can not write a note to HER.
> HE is not able to talk with HER.
> So HE is the disabled!
>
> SHE can write her note to HIM.
> SHE can figure how to talk with HIM.
> SHE knows how to teach HIM to talk.
> So SHE is ABLED or ENABLED.

HE passes HER many times.
HE neglects HER so easy.
HE can not think what will HE say to HER.
So HE is disabled.

HE see HER able to write HER note.
HE can read HER writing.
HE learns from HER how to Print On Palm.
So HE is abled to talk with HER.

Then both disabled are gone, gone.
No more "disabled."
Both are enabled!

To this document Leslie had appended a footnote, a single sentence. "Many non-DeafBlind people are true disabled to the DeafBlind worlds," it read, "unless they are willing to learn how to work with them."

At home, Leslie constructed a fantastic hive of an office, planned it in such a way as to place a thousand things within easy reach of his chair. From his command center, he hammered out emails bearing witness to injustices, advocating for change, and sharing jokes, poems, and stories; he co-moderated DeafBlind Minnesota, a vital email listserv resource; he organized weekly DeafBlind Club gatherings, where he loved to play chess, with chessboards he designed; and he carried out his duties as off-again and on-again president of Minnesota DeafBlind Association, an organization he helped to establish in 1977. A God-loving man, he attended Sunday meetings and poured out his soul, often in the form of ASL poetry. He knew the Twin Cities bus system like the back of his hand, and he carried a binder full of printed notes for the drivers instructing them as to where he wanted to get off. He couldn't resist tinkering with everything, including the universally accepted and unquestioned white cane. The unique padded cane he designed brought him notoriety. And he wrote a poem, in English, in which the speaker turns out to be his cane complaining about its owner. "The True Story: The DeafBlind Man Abuses Me" opens with these lines:

> The DeafBlind man (aka DB) adopted me and
>   use me for no reasons.
> I really shock he abuses me all times.
> Even he hang me on the hook.
> Even he leaves me lone on anywhere.

Midway through the poem, a hilarious passage:

> I wish I have 2 arms and 2 feets.
> Then I could run away from him.
> I could have some help.
> I have no way to do.

In the poem's brilliant closing lines, before the speaker's identity is spelled out, there is a beautiful gesture of reconciliation, of resignation. The cane-speaker and the DeafBlind man blend together:

> It seems DB can not
> kill or destroy me.
> He keeps me live and strong.
> I learned to accept what DB does to me.
> He labels me, "THE WHITE CANE."

During one DeafBlind Club gathering, Leslie turned to me and asked how I said "mother" and "father" in ASL. To say both together is clear enough to read tactilely, but in isolation, just "mother" here and "father" there, it's impossible to tell the difference. The ASL speaker places those words at their chin for "mother" and at their temple for "father," which is visually distinct but ambiguous when felt by hand. After some discussion, we hit upon a possible solution, saying "mommy" and "father" or, alternatively, "mother" and "daddy." We had similar conversations to puzzle out the problems ASL presented to us as tactile people. Protactile hadn't arrived yet, but those discussions were a harbinger.

At the age of sixty-six, Leslie learned he had stage-four cancer. He took the news in stride, and declined any treatment. He said he was grateful to God for giving him time to prepare. He continued attending DeafBlind Club and visiting me to play chess until it was time for him to go to a terminal care facility. The first time I entered his room there, I had to smile. Leslie immediately showed me around the world he had built there, not unlike the one in our basement all those years ago. He had hammered and screwed together shelving, set up tables just so, and put down strategic rugs. It was a cozy place in the middle of an otherwise sterile environment.

We continued playing chess, our knees snugly interlocked under a narrow table. I noted the increasing tremors in his legs and hands. He told me that all his life it had been imperative to have some struggle, a challenge. Chess provided one source of the friction he craved. It was no contradiction but part of Leslie's gambit, his art of life, that he greeted death with a sanguine calm.

His funeral was jarring. I wasn't the only one upset by how hearing and sighted people were orchestrating the service.

Speakers stood in front of rows of people, and the DeafBlind attendees were separated from one another, each one sitting next to an interpreter who relayed the proceedings. Leslie was so amazing, the speakers all said. Which was true, but not in the way that they meant. They had no idea. Afterward, at the luncheon, a friend turned to me, stricken. "Promise me," she said, "you won't let them do that for my funeral."

I hesitated to make such a promise. After all, we hadn't been in a position to give our beloved outlaw king a proper funeral. The world wasn't ours enough. But something told me that I could afford to make that promise. "Yes," I said. "We'll do it right for you."

PART ONE

KNOWING AND BEING KNOWN

AGAINST ACCESS

An autographed game-used baseball—bearing personalized inscriptions by two players on the Minnesota Twins, Chuck Knoblauch and Hall of Famer Kirby Puckett—is the sole surviving physical evidence of a childhood consumed by sports. Although it's not inaccurate to say I was born DeafBlind, since I have the progressive-blindness condition known as Usher syndrome, it's often more helpful to say I was born Deaf and gradually became blind, growing into my DeafBlind identity. As a kid, I had tens of thousands of baseball cards that I would strain my eyes to read. My shrines to that time are all gone now, save for this one baseball. I never thought I would entertain the idea of giving it away, but here I am. Should I keep it? It doesn't take up much space. But what does it mean to me now? It's like a moon rock, a lonely object out of space and time.

Jim Fuller, a staff writer for the Minneapolis *Star Tribune*, was the one who, beaming, presented me with the baseball. He first came to our house to interview my father about his efforts to establish a bilingual Deaf charter school. Jim soon discovered that I was a sports fanatic. We got to scribbling notes back and forth about our beloved Twins. Jim said he would have a surprise for me the next time he stopped by.

Although he gave me the baseball in the summer of 1993, it evokes my happiest sports memory, which took place two years earlier, when the Twins played in the greatest World Series ever. When Puckett walloped it out of the park to take us into Game Seven, I could hardly breathe. Then it was John Smoltz and Jack Morris taking turns on the mound. In the bottom of the tenth, with Smoltz out of the game and Alejandro Pena in relief, a Twin stretched a bloop into a double. A few at-bats later the bases were loaded, and when the next batter made contact, the first tore off. As Dan Gladden, a.k.a. Clinton Daniel Gladden III, a.k.a. the Dazzle Man, flew down the home stretch, the universe, the whole world, my very being rushed toward him. Nothing can do justice to the moment he leaped and landed on home plate except witnessing it with your own eyes. Any attempt to describe it is futile. Description can only serve a roundabout purpose.

It took me a long time to realize this. I continued to follow sports after I could no longer witness events with my eyes. It pleased me to believe I still had access through sports news, box scores, occasionally enlisting someone to sit next to me and relay games, and, above all, reading fine sportswriting. Wasn't baseball synonymous with literature? It therefore baffled me when I found myself keeping up with sports less and less. I skipped the Super Bowl a few years after the television screen ceased to be legible, breaking a tradition going back as far as memory. I unsubscribed from *ESPN: The Magazine* even though the list of magazines available in hard-copy Braille is short and precious. Then it was down to one sportswriter, Bill

Simmons, a most diverting raconteur. I accepted that I now required good writing to maintain my interest in sports. But even the Sports Guy's columns began to lose their charm after a while. What was going on? At first, what I read or listened to live through an interpreter teemed with players I had worshipped with my own eyes. I knew their faces, their tics, the way they licked their upper lips or groaned or stared or gasped in horror or with joy. As they faded into retirement, there was less and less poetry in what I gathered, replaced by new and strange and meaningless names. Direct experience goes a long way. It meant that sports did resonate with me for years after my last eloquent encounter. But without direct experience, I learned I couldn't access the same life.

Disability rights activists have long fought for access, most often in the form of basic and unobtrusive accommodations. Today, billions of dollars are poured into projects seeking to increase inclusion. It's not that I don't appreciate it when a restaurant has a Braille menu. A device attached to a streetlight post that vibrates when it's safe to cross the street is huge for me. Programs created in the name of access make it possible for me to write this essay. Ramps, elevators, wide doorways, flashing lights, railings, benches, assistants, care workers, and myriad technologies make all the difference in the world. But the way those things are lobbied for, funded, designed, implemented, and used revolves around the assumption that there's only one world and ignores realms of possibility nestled within those same modes.

The question I am asked most frequently by hearing and sighted people is "How can I make my—website, gallery exhibit, film, performance, concert, whatever—accessible to you?" Companies, schools, nonprofits, and state and federal agencies approach me and other DeafBlind people all the time, demanding, "How do we make it more accessible?"

Such a frenzy around access is suffocating. I want to tell them, *Listen, I don't care about your whatever.* But the desperation on their breath holds me dumbfounded. The arrogance is astounding. Why is it always about them? Why is it about their including or not including us? Why is it never about us and whether or not *we* include *them*?

In my community, we are in the midst of a revolution. We have our first truly tactile language, called Protactile. We insist on doing everything our way, fumbling around, groping along, touching everything and everyone. We are messing with traditional spaces, rearranging them to suit us better, rather than the other way around. The Protactile movement is obsessed with direct experience. As Robert Sirvage, a DeafBlind architect, put it in a recent conversation, the question we begin with is not "How do we make it more accessible?" Instead, we start by asking, "What feels beautiful?" When hearing and sighted people join us, they pick up Protactile and learn how to work and socialize with us in our space. They often find themselves closing their eyes, either literally or by dimming their visual processing, because sight isn't necessary. Bodies in contact become as normal to them as they are to us.

When the word "access" comes up, it usually refers to tools or avenues that complement the sensory experience people already enjoy. Captions for movies, TV shows, and videos are excellent examples. They are said to provide access for Deaf people, who, I need to stress, already have a relationship with the images flitting across the screen. When blind people ask for audio descriptions, this accommodation merely supplements what they already hear. For example, the audio description might helpfully note that "the king is waving his sword, his cloak billowing in the wind" when a king shouts, "Follow me, ye good knights!" But then there are the efforts to feed captions into Braille displays so DeafBlind people can have "access" to radio, TV, and film. This isn't complementary access. It's a replica, divorced entirely from the original. This is how we frequently find accessibility features—as sorry excuses for what occasioned them in the first place. Access itself is too often all we have, a dead end, leading nowhere: captions without images, lyrics without music, raised lines without color, labels without objects, descriptions without anchors.

In the United States, there are tens of thousands of American Sign Language interpreters, who are trained to facilitate communication in the most accurate and impartial manner possible. You could say they are human captions. The rigor with which they strive to translate between ASL and English, and between various cultural frames of reference, may be a wonderful way for sighted Deaf people to gain access—which is to say, *complementary* access—to many settings. But ASL interpreters are an atrocity for DeafBlind people, constantly inserting themselves between us and other people in order to facilitate conversations, but instead getting in the way of direct connections. This was one of the things that unwittingly helped give birth to Protactile in 2007.

Protactile took root only when a group of DeafBlind leaders in Seattle decided to conduct meetings and workshops without any interpreters. DeafBlind community members were shocked by how well those events went, with participants communicating directly and rotating from cluster to cluster. This success emboldened us to break many taboos related to touch, including touching one another's bodies instead of just moving our hands in the air. A grammar soon developed to coordinate all that contact. A new language was born. It's no accident that this explosion occurred when we took a break from the most prevalent manifestation of access in our midst: ASL interpreters.

My experiences on September 11, 2001, provide an illustration of why, before the Protactile era, it was so frustrating to work with interpreters. I went to my postcolonial literature class at the University of Minnesota without having read any news online earlier that day. I found my two ASL interpreters already there. They immediately asked me, "Did you hear about an airplane hitting two poles?"

I laughed. "No, but that's funny. So today they'll be talking about Rudyard Kipling's *Kim*. How about we give Kipling this ASL name and Kim this ASL name? To distinguish between the author and the character? Good?"

A long pause.

I repeated, "Good?"

"Yes . . . that's fine," they said. They were acting strange. When the professor arrived, the energy was weird. He asked if everyone was all right. Did anyone have family in New York? Did anyone need to leave class?

It wasn't until hours later that I read the news and understood what had happened. People must have been upset and crying. All the TV screens running the same footage over and over. And my interpreters had failed—miserably—to convey any of it to me in a meaningful way. Why? Because they were there only to "provide access," primarily to the spoken English content of the class.

Fast-forward to one of the Protactile movement's biggest achievements to date: creating a new kind of interpreter. In 2017, we launched the DeafBlind Interpreting National Training and Resource Center and began hosting weeklong immersion trainings for interpreters, led by DeafBlind Protactile experts. When my colleagues and I started developing the program, we quickly realized that the point wasn't just to help interpreters become fluent in Protactile. It had to facilitate a complete reinvention of their role. Instead of providing "accurate and objective information" in a way that unsuccessfully attempts to create a replica of how they're experiencing the world, Protactile interpreters must be our informants, our partners, our accomplices. Typically, ASL interpreters are system-centered, leashed to a platform or classroom or meeting room or video call, jerked into action every time someone speaks in English. There's usually a power imbalance, such as between a hearing teacher and a Deaf student, a hearing doctor and a Deaf patient, or a hearing boss and a Deaf employee. With this power imbalance in mind, we can understand why ASL interpreters often "belong" to the hearing party more than the Deaf party. This is problematic for sighted Deaf people, but it is devastating for DeafBlind people. Protactile interpreters, by contrast, are consumer-centered, firmly aligned with us, following our lead as we figure out how to hack into situations. We recognize that there's little value for us in spaces where people stay physically apart and the built environment does not invite contact. The question in working with an interpreter for us then becomes: What do *we* want to get out of it? What we want is never what hearing and sighted people plan or propose to do, because they never ask us, "What shall we do together? How do you want to do this?" They merely wish to include us.

A story to illustrate what has changed with this new role for interpreters: Early in the COVID-19 pandemic, a Deaf-Blind friend told me about her recent experience working with a Protactile interpreter I'd helped train. She had a doctor's appointment, and the Protactile interpreter met her at the entrance to the building.

"Wow," the interpreter said as they entered the waiting room, "everyone here is tense and talking about COVID. The TV over there: it's on COVID. Do you want me to relay that, on the TV, or eavesdrop on what the doctor over there is saying to a cluster of people . . . something about masks?"

My friend dismissed it all with a sweep of her hand across the interpreter's chest. "Not interested. So how was your trip to—"

"Yes, yes," he interjected, "we can talk about my trip, but I just want to make sure. Do you know what COVID is?"

"I have no idea."

"Whoa. Okay, okay, okay. Listen, COVID is *earthshaking* news." He grasped her shoulders to mock-shake them for emphasis.

After he explained COVID-19, my friend was awed and now wanted to know what the TV was saying, and had many questions for her doctor.

Here, the Protactile interpreter operated as my friend's partner, making subjective yet vital contributions. When he found her dismissal of COVID-19 odd, he pressed her on the topic. An ASL interpreter would never have done that, unless they allowed their instincts to overrule their training.

When I teach ASL interpreters that they must share their opinions and assessments, they always protest, "But I don't want to influence the DeafBlind person!"

"If you're worried about influencing us," I reply, "you give yourself too much credit and us too little."

Another thing ASL interpreters habitually do is describe the whole of things. Upon entering a room, for example, they stop and say, "This is a midsize room with a few tables, here, there, and over there. There are . . . let's see, one, two, three, four, five, six, okay, six windows—"

Here I stop them. "Why are you telling me, telling me,

telling me things? Your job isn't to deliver this whole room to me on a silver platter. I don't want the silver platter. I want to *attack* this room. I want to own it, just like how the sighted people here own it. Or, if the room isn't worth owning, then I want to grab whatever I find worth stealing. C'mon, let's start over. What we'll do is start to touch things and people here, together, while we provide running commentaries and feedback to each other."

Although I travel places and enter spaces alone all the time, interacting with the environment and people I encounter according to how things unfold, it's often nice to have a sighted co-navigator, such as an interpreter. It may mean being able to approach someone who is not standing where I'd typically be exploring, along a wall or from landmark to landmark. If the person doesn't know Protactile, the interpreter can translate my quick explanation of what I need them to do—put their hand on my hand and give me feedback with their other hand—and why I am using their upper chest or arm or leg to describe something. I can establish that contact with strangers without an interpreter, but it may take a few false starts before they "get it." They may forget to give me adequate feedback, so the interpreter will relay to me their reactions to our exchange.

Giving quick reads without getting bogged down in details is an important skill for a spy doing live reconnaissance. But ASL interpreters are at first inhibited by notions of neutrality and objectivity. They start by offering something like "Walking by over there is a tall, thin, light-skinned person with curly dark hair down to here, wearing a white tank top, blue jeans, and brown boots . . ." They're pleased that they've avoided race and gender.

"No, no, no." I brush my hands back and forth across their

arm in vigorous negation. "That's not the way to do it. The very same description could be applied to a gorgeous Latina in chic, expensive boots who oozes money, *or* to a pasty, rangy white man, hair a mess, boots falling apart, maybe looking angry. Like, they're the opposite of each other? Yet they share the same sanitized description."

Because of their fear of bias, I discuss four implicit safety nets to help them feel better about uttering an assessment:

> FIRST, we're not so fragile that saying something wrong will topple us. We know what we are doing. We—not they—are in charge of our missions. Responsibility lies with us, not with them.

> SECOND, I tell them a story about the best interpreter I worked with before the Protactile era. He was a volunteer rather than a professional interpreter, and because of this, his commentary was so unvarnished that I picked up a *ton* through him. He also happened to be a racist and misogynistic Deaf man, but I was able to separate his bias from the information he gave me. I ask my interpreting students, "Are you an unabashed bigot? No? Then you have that much less to be worried about." This interpreter wasn't good at his job because he was bigoted; rather, he was good because he functioned as an open channel of information, and so everything in his brain was revealed, his bias along with it. "You don't want his bigotry," I tell my students, "but you want his talent for not thinking twice."

> THIRD, if they're so terrified of letting slip their own opinions, I tell them, then they should consider what I call "collective subjectivity." Suppose a hundred sighted people see

someone sauntering into a room. In that Gladwellian blink of an eye, they all come to a hundred slightly different conclusions based on their own life experiences. An interpreter may happen to be a fashion maven and know the person's expensive-looking boots are knockoffs, for example. But nevertheless, there will be certain cultural signifiers that are recognizable to the majority of those hundred people, however correct they may or may not be. The question is: What is it that is being broadcast to the collective? We don't have time to listen to a long deposition, the thousand words that a picture is rumored to be worth, for us to reach a reasonable conclusion—*if* we can even reach such a conclusion, since ours is not a visual world. It's so helpful to have an aide de camp to tell us whether someone is receptive to us or if our charm is being wasted.

FOURTH, there's the Gladwellian blink of an eye, and then there's the Gladwellian—or Clarkian!—slide or pat or jiggle of the hand. By bumping into, sniffing, tapping, brushing past, we are gathering intelligence of our own. That's why we shouldn't stop while our interpreter attempts to construct a replica but should instead continue picking up important information that may confirm, contradict, or qualify what an interpreter contributes.

After nudging two hundred–plus ASL interpreters through the travails of rebirth as Protactile interpreters, I began to understand why people who work around access cling to the concept of accuracy. This commitment to accuracy, to perfect replication, is a commitment to the status quo. We are expected to leave it untouched, or, if it must be altered, then to do so as little as possible. Access, then, is akin to nonreciprocal assimilation, with its two possible outcomes: death by fitting in or death by failing to fit in. The Protactile movement is the latest pulling away from replication. In Deaf history, generations of hearing educators have tried to use sign language expressly to represent the dominant written language, first by finger spelling letter for letter and, after tiring of this, word for word. It was always shaped around the dominant language and never about what *real* sign language had to offer. One unintentionally hilarious attempt at accuracy was a system called Signing Exact English. In blind history, reading by touch started with raised lines that followed, exactly, the lines of printed letters. When the lines proved painfully slow to trace with one's fingers, sighted educators grudgingly allowed for them to be more blocky and a bit easier to feel. Braille—as a different world, a world of dots as opposed to lines—was available as an option, but sighted educators persisted in wanting something as close to print as possible. Even though Braille is now universally accepted, it is still being treated as merely a way to represent print, rather than being its own code and co-language. At stake isn't accuracy, but whose accuracy.

In recent years, there has been a rush on the internet to supply image descriptions and to call out those who don't. This may be an example of community accountability at work, but it's striking to observe that those doing the fiercest calling out or correcting are sighted people. Such efforts are largely self-defeating. I cannot count the times I stopped reading a video transcript because it started with a dense word picture. Even if a description is short and well done, I often wish there were no description at all. Get to the point, already! How ironic that striving after access can actually create a barrier. When I pointed this out during one of my seminars, a participant made us all laugh by doing a parody: "Mary is wearing a green, blue, and red striped shirt; every fourth stripe also has a purple dot the size of a pea in it, and there are forty-seven stripes—"

"You're killing me," I said. "I can't take any more of that!"

Now serious, she said it was clear to her that none of that stuff about Mary's clothes mattered, at least if her clothes weren't the point. What mattered most about the image was that Mary was holding her diploma and smiling. "But," she wondered, "do I say, 'Mary has a huge smile on her face as she shows her diploma' or 'Mary has an exuberant smile' or 'showing her teeth in a smile and her eyes are crinkled at the edges'?"

It's simple. "Mary has a huge smile on her face" is the best one. It's the don't-second-guess-yourself option. My thinking around this issue is enriched by the philosopher Brian Massumi's concept of "esqueness." He exemplifies it by discussing a kid who plays a tiger:

> One look at a tiger, however fleeting and incomplete, whether it be in the zoo or in a book or in a film or video, and presto! the child is tigerized . . . *The perception itself is a vital gesture.* The child immediately sets about, not imitating the tiger's substantial form as he saw it, but rather giving it life—giving it more life. The child plays the tiger in situations in which the child has never seen a tiger. More than that, it plays the tiger in situations no *tiger* has ever seen, in which no earthly tiger has ever set paw.

Just like how the child and an actual tiger are not one bit alike, the words "Mary has a huge smile on her face" have nothing in common with the picture of Mary holding her diploma. Yet the tiger announces something to the world, its essence, and a kid can become tiger-ized and be tiger-esque, their every act shouting, *I am a tiger.* The picture of Mary at her graduation is shouting something, and the words "Mary has a huge smile on her face" are also shouting something. It is at the level beyond each actuality, in the swirl that each stirs up, that the two meet.

We would do well to abandon the pretense that it's possible to reproduce base things in realms other than those that gave birth to them. Instead, we can leave those things well enough alone where they belong, or, moved by possibilities, we can transgress, translate, and transform them. We can give foreign things new purposes, which may be slightly or extremely different from their original intent. Take the card game UNO, one of the games widely available in a Braille version. The standard cards have dots at the corner that say things like "Y5" for a yellow card with the number five. In practice, playing the game with the Brailled cards is painfully slow. If Protactile hadn't given us permission to rip sighted norms into shreds, I would still be fingering those dots like a fool. The way to go is with textured shapes, as in our homemade version of UNO, called Textures and Shapes. In this Protactile version, you feel the player ahead of you hesitate and make a joking gesture before depositing a velvet star. Now the attention shifts to you, with some hands feeling yours as you deliberate, while a couple of knees tauntingly jostle your knees. Should you unload your velvet square or rayon star? But the transformation doesn't end there. Ideally, there are up to four players, who can feel everything at all times if they wanted to follow the action or chatter in three-way Protactile while the fourth attends to their turn. With four players as the ideal limit, there are somewhat fewer textured shapes than there are UNO cards in a set, and there are further tweaks to the rules. And the "wild card" is a delightful eruption of fabrics! It's a different game, and one that is naturally more inclusive than UNO could ever be. Our environment has endless potential for life. For centuries, however, much of our vitality was forbidden. We were forced to stick with the effects of the hearing and sighted world. Now, though, we are all in varying stages of flight.

Sighted and hearing people have always had a hard time accepting that we are happy for them. Why have they never been happy for us? They wish only to be happy for themselves through us. Part of the fear many of them feel when encountering DeafBlind people comes from the way we naturally decline so much of what they cherish. They seek relief from this anxiety by insisting that we take in their world. Then they ask us a rhetorical question: "It's great, isn't it, this world of ours?" This is the awful function of access: to make others happy at our expense. Until Protactile plunged us into the churning currents of *being*, we didn't know what we were giving up by consuming access. And sighted and hearing people didn't know what they were missing out on by not entering our world.

In April 2020, I made a small but telling gesture. An online journal wanted a photo of me to go along with three poems it was publishing. I had long wanted to do something about this photo business, even if there were an image description to make it "accessible." Since I don't see author images, I'm not immersed in the conventions of that particular species of media. So why should I provide a headshot as if I knew what it conveyed and knew that it was what I want to convey? To my surprise, the magazine agreed to my request: No photo! Instead, a few words, a tactile description suggestive of what it's like to touch me in person. I now tinker with it like I do my bio. My current line goes something like this: "Short hair of feline softness. Warm and smooth hands. A scent of patchouli. Flutters betray his exhilaration."

A few months later, I went aflutter when Terra Edwards,

a dear hearing-sighted friend and a leading Protactile researcher, told me she wanted to thenceforth avoid images as much as possible for the materials we publish related to Protactile. Our research team set up a website called the Protactile Research Network. No pictures, icons, or graphics. Text only! Under "People," where our bios and CVs reside, there is a "tactile impression" of each member of the team. I love Terra's: "Strong hands. Heats up in conversation. Frequent and enthusiastic tapping likely."

And here is Hayley Broadway, a DeafBlind researcher currently working with DeafBlind children on Protactile language acquisition: "Wears fashionable, textured attire. Wiggles her fingers on you when she is deep in thought. When you talk to her, you feel a steady stream of taps and squeezes. Sometimes, when she is really excited, she slaps you. Engage at your own risk."

As always, Jelica Nuccio—my dearest friend, personal hero, and rock of the Protactile movement—has the last hug: "Her stories are smooth and come with the scent of lavender. She draws you in slowly and then grips. When she laughs on you, you can't help but laugh too."

ALWAYS BE CONNECTED

I

It's an exciting time to be DeafBlind. The single most important development in DeafBlind history is in full swing. Called the Protactile movement, it's moving through our community like nothing has ever done before.

Launched in Seattle, which has perhaps the most active local DeafBlind community in the United States, Protactile is difficult to describe with its many political, linguistic, and practical elements. As innovative as it is, many of these ideas and practices are quite old. After all, Protactile grows out of what is natural to us as DeafBlind people. Jelica Nuccio, founder of Tactile Communications, and aj granda, an activist, put it all together, giving it a holistic, philosophical package and the needed wallop.

DeafBlind people have typically been in a bubble when communicating with others. Let's take a look at a page from Wally Thomas's wonderful 1960 memoir, *Life in My Hands*.

He was deafened and blinded during World War Two while serving on Great Britain's bomb disposal unit. After he accidentally exploded a clump of T.N.T. he underwent a whirlwind series of surgeries. About one of these experiences, he wrote: "During a lucid period I was told I was going to have an operation. I felt pretty good that day. I said: "What is it to be this time, a boy or a girl?" No one laughed. Some people don't appreciate a brilliant sense of humor. They just stuck a needle in my arm."

Later, when he came to, Thomas asked for water. They wrote on his palm, "You had your operation four hours ago and the triplets are doing fine."

Ah, so they did appreciate Wally's wit! But they didn't have a way to convey their laughter to him as he was telling his joke. When hearing and sighted people laugh, they assume this fact is conveyed to everyone in their presence. The needle that went into Wally's arm didn't burst the bubble. He was able to tell jokes but didn't know if they landed or not, at least not right away. Others could penetrate the bubble to communicate with him, but as soon as it was Wally's turn to speak, he was back in the bubble, talking into empty space. For the rest of his long and active life—he traveled much, wrote, and was the subject of two popular songs—he could only trust or imagine that others were listening and reacting.

When I started listening to American Sign Language tactilely in high school, I found it liberating. I had been relying on my increasingly blind eyes, and the turn to tactile communication was like a breath of fresh air. Best of all, others proved to be happy to communicate with me in this way, whereas before they had been confused or annoyed by my requirements related to lighting, distance, signing space, color of clothes, and contrasting backgrounds.

As wonderful as it was to make this change, new problems emerged. The person with whom I was talking might suddenly look away because someone across the room waved for their attention. I kept speaking as if nothing had happened. If they nodded, I didn't know that. If they laughed, I didn't know until I finished my joke and it was their turn, whereupon they might say, "Ha ha!" I often asked yes-or-no questions, seeking feedback to help me proceed further, only to have this be mistaken for their turn. Or, if I snatched my hand back to continue, they felt I was being rude.

Thus, many of my conversations with sighted people resembled conversations on the TTY—a typewriter phone that Deaf people used before the Internet, texting, and videophones replaced it—where one person typed one message at a time before typing "GA," short for "go ahead," indicating that it was the other party's turn to type. Such conversations don't have the same flow of information, feedback looping, and cues that sighted and hearing people enjoy when talking with each other in person.

Also, the feeling that I was talking to a wall meant I sensed my native expressiveness fall flat. If you don't have feedback, it is harder to keep on ranting or rhapsodizing. This problem sometimes made it impossible for me to give a presentation. I knew I had an audience, most likely an appreciative one, but I could not feed off their energy. If I was lucky, I might have enough inner vitality to carry the presentation.

Whenever I talked with fellow tactile listeners, however, I felt alive. It was always a joy to feel their hands on mine and to feel their every reaction. Our conversations flowed with electricity, and we often talked at once, whole words and phrases overlapping and chasing one another. I felt my most authentic, most eloquent, most myself.

What hadn't occurred to me but did to Jelica and aj was to ask that everyone, sighted or hearing or Deaf or blind or DeafBlind, enter and stay in this tactile space with us. To banish forever the bubble that used to separate DeafBlind people from the people we talked to. That is what Protactile is all about. It gives everyone the principles and norms to create and maintain such spaces, where we can enjoy equal access to information and participate fully.

When hearing people want to socialize with Deaf people, they have to become Deaf themselves, by speaking ASL, by listening visually, by giving visual cues, and by refraining from intrusive hearing behaviors. Otherwise, Deaf and hearing people wouldn't be able to share the same spaces. This is widely understood and practiced. So the expectation that hearing and sighted people become DeafBlind themselves, by speaking Protactile, shouldn't come to anyone as a shock. "When in Rome, do as the Romans do." It's an old idea, but one that was never applied to DeafBlind communities until Protactile put tactile reciprocity at the heart of a new way of life.

II

In 2013, Jelica and aj came to Minnesota to lead a four-day training for eight of us regional DeafBlind community leaders. We assembled in a hotel in Bloomington, bumping into each other and hugging each other in greeting. When Jelica and I found each other, we jumped together. We had gone through many adventures together, including cycling along the Pacific Coast from San Francisco to Los Angeles, but it had been five years since we'd last touched each other. She wasted no time. "Protactile now, Protactile now, Protactile now," she chanted. I showed my assent by playfully rushing both of us toward the training room. When we entered, I was delighted to discover there weren't any interpreters there to relay a presentation from a platform. Instead, everyone sat in clusters of twos or threes, interacting directly and rotating so we had some turns sitting with Jelica and other turns with aj and turns with fellow participants.

For the first round, I sat down with Jaz Herbers, a DeafBlind man very new to our community, having only recently gone tactile. Soon aj joined us. The first thing she said was, "You know how eyes are oh so sacred to Deaf people? And hearing people have those tiny holes at the sides of their heads? Well, Protactile philosophy is simple. We DeafBlind people *touch*." She said the last word with a dramatic swoop of her hands, which landed on our respective legs with a resounding slap.

We touch. Of course. Did we need to be told that? Yes, we did. The oppression we'd been subjected to made sure we didn't know what it meant to be tactile. We shouldn't have needed permission to touch, but we did. To touch was a huge favor to ask, and we trembled whenever we reached out too much. In 2007, things came to a head in Seattle. Through a unique series of circumstances there was a sudden shortage of interpreters. At first this led Jelica, then the director of Deaf-Blind Service Center, and aj, who worked with her, to cancel or postpone meetings that had typically required interpreters. They soon decided to go ahead with those meetings without interpreters. This was how Protactile emerged—not for the first time, as it had always been inside of us, but this time emerging to stay and flourish. The success of those meetings that relied on direct communication among DeafBlind people revealed the depth of our mistaken assumption that sight was necessary. And how we were already, subconsciously, fed up with trying to do things the sighted way. Fed up with inter-preters always facilitating communication. Fed up with Sup-port Service Providers—paid sighted guides—intervening whenever we reached out to feel something, or fumbled around, or groped along. Sighted people were always swoop-ing in and saying, "Let me help you with that" or "Stay here, I'll get it for you" or "Wait."

So Jelica and aj began doing classes, meetings, and activities without sighted people controlling everything under the cover of providing access and assistance. Some DeafBlind folks balked. "I need an interpreter! How will I know what the oth-ers are saying?" One DeafBlind man, arriving at the location of a workshop in the early days of the movement, entered and waited near the door. And waited. And waited. He stood there until someone in the workshop, already in progress, needed to go to the restroom. She bumped into him and said, "Hey you! We were starting to wonder if you'd show up. What are you doing standing here?"

"Waiting for someone to come guide me," he said. "Why didn't anyone come get me?"

"Don't be silly. You have to go ahead and feel around. Come on, let me show you how. You can follow this wall, and veer away here, walk around the room to find out if anyone is here. And here you go!" They had bumped into the group, which greeted him and pulled him into a new world.

Without sighted people helping them to conduct the work-shop in a sighted format by having many interpreters in the room to relay to each DeafBlind person what a presenter was saying, the group quickly figured out how to do it differently. They formed clusters of two or three people each, and partici-pants switched from one cluster to another. The Protactile way to do meetings, classes, and presentations was born. No longer do we require interpreters to be able to present, teach, or share information within our community.

That was the beginning of a long series of breakthroughs. Our centering of touch forced us to reconsider everything and to take nothing for granted. No one invented Protactile. It kept on evolving, often without us realizing it. One of the most astonishing things that emerged was a new language. Its first tender shoots had come up immediately. In 2010, a Ph.D. candidate in linguistic anthropology and a longtime friend of our community named Terra Edwards secured permission to film a workshop in Seattle. She noticed patterns in how DeafBlind people were communicating with each other and was blown away.

"No way!" Jelica told Terra. "Protactile is NOT a language!"

When Terra convinced Jelica that, yes, here was an emerging language, Jelica understood that Protactile was something much bigger than previously thought. Jelica and aj began traveling to share Protactile. Their trip to Minnesota in 2013 to teach me and seven of my colleagues was their first effort to train people who would, in our turn, help spread Protactile farther. And we did just that.

But what to teach is always changing, because things are still evolving so fast. One day sighted people were touching our speaking arms so they could give us feedback. The next day sighted and DeafBlind people alike placed a hand on our main speaking hand, meaning that we no longer communicated to sighted people differently than we did to each other. One day we were moving our hands in what we call "air space," with our interlocutors doing tactile reception, yes, but the words themselves were made in the area between us. The next day whole flocks of word-birds fell out of the sky. They landed into what we call "contact space," our hands patting, brushing over, and making minute and varied impressions on our listeners' chests, arms, and legs. One day all the languages in the world were spoken with a tongue or two hands. The next day this was no longer the case. Protactile asserted itself as a language in which one person cannot speak alone, in which another body is required, in which four articulators conspire to agitate the universe.

How to explain it all? How to define the indefinable? In their landmark 2017 paper, "Protactile Principles," aj and Jelica wrote:

> Protactile philosophy has grown out of the realization that DeafBlind people's intuitions about tactile communication are stronger than the intuitions sighted people have. This realization has changed the way we communicate with each other, the way we work with interpreters, and more generally, the way we live.

My attempt at encapsulating what Protactile means considers three braided complements:

MOVEMENT. It is a DeafBlind-led movement that seeks to make increasing claims on the world, to change it, to do things in our own way, and to build spaces of our own that we then welcome others into. Protactile philosophy holds that vision and hearing are not required to live and thrive.

PRACTICES. To apply this philosophy, we are discovering how we want to live, learn, navigate, and set up spaces. The process requires that we challenge and throw out many norms and values imposed by sighted society.

LANGUAGE. None of this would be possible without our own language, which has rapidly evolved into not only a language in its own right but also one in an entirely new modality. Its salient features include the use of four linguistic hands, the speaker's hands together with the receiver's hands; the use of contact space, or the receiver's body; and the use of taps, presses, squeezes, lines traced, and other movements.

Helpful though this breakdown may be, it fails to convey the sheer sensation of movement, of everything swirling, surging, exploding. There was no time for reflection. There was time only for experience, at least for a while, until words could begin to describe it.

III

When I came back home after that four-day training with Jelica and aj, my family—which includes my Deaf sighted partner, Adrean, and our three hearing-sighted kids—began to implement Protactile practices. But "implement" is the wrong word. Yes, there was a conscious decision, yet how it played out was a dream, one that is still unfolding.

One of the first shifts occurred in our kitchen. It used to be that Adrean and I could not be in it at the same time. How she went about cooking as a sighted person was completely different than the way I went about cooking as a tactile person, and we had believed it best to have it be one person in there at a time. Traditionally, sighted people gave us a wide berth whenever we were at work. For us, it meant losing opportunities. For example, I might be peeling apples while remembering that I needed to tell Adrean something, unaware that she was at the moment walking through the kitchen to throw something in the trash can. She might pass behind me again on her way out, and that particular thought might be gone forever.

Protactile changed that. It gave Adrean and me a way to inhabit the kitchen at the same time, by going in the opposite direction of "giving each other space." We began to touch each other much more, brushing our hands across each other's back as we passed or maintaining contact while we were doing different things, such as with our feet touching while she mixed salad greens and I plied the frying pan. I often slide my arm down against her leg as I squat to pull out a mixing bowl from a lower cabinet. She often purposely moves her arm against my neck to reach something in a cupboard above my head.

At the dining table, we no longer sit around the table to make a pretty Norman Rockwell picture. Doing so in the past had meant I could only talk comfortably with the person sitting next to me on either side. It meant someone had to relay to me what someone out of my reach was saying. We now eat in clusters. We developed new habits. We all created Protactile names so we could identify ourselves to each other. By placing our name on any part of another's body, we let them know who it is that is passing by, has entered, is leaving, or will be right back.

We learned, too, that we could feel what someone is doing without it being taken as our wishing to speak or it being taken as an interruption. Protactile has given me a way to observe Adrean hard at work weaving strips of paper for her famous homemade greeting cards, or one of my kids playing a video game, or to eavesdrop on a conversation already in progress. Before Protactile arrived, sighted people always froze when I touched them. They shot out their hands, saying "Yes?" or "What do you need?" or, worst of all, "Hold!" I felt bad for interrupting them. But in the new world we are building, there's no such thing as interruption, only observing or joining in.

When I began teaching Protactile, first in my local community and later on the national and international levels, I realized that the one thing we had to hammer in is what my colleague at the Protactile Language Interpreting National Education Center, CM Hall, put into a nifty acronym: ABC. Always Be Connected. This doesn't mean we have to be glued together all the time. But it does mean a context in which we have psychic rubber bands connecting us that we can stretch when we move away. The default is that we make contact and maintain contact. Terra, who is now a principal Protactile researcher, refers to the concept as "co-presence," something that hearing and sighted people take for granted but that had been sorely lacking in our lives.

A strange phenomenon of the era before Protactile is that the people who enjoyed DeafBlind events the most were sighted people. A sighted person only had to look around, see many people, and think, "What a lovely time we all are having!" It is difficult for a sighted person to realize that their presence doesn't register with us unless and until they connect directly with us. So a major concern of the Protactile movement is to establish co-presence. Protactile etiquette demands that we cluster together and seek to have clusters touch one another in some way. Nicole and I may be having a conversation, for example, while Jelica and Heather are having another. The two pairs may be in touch side by side or back to back. If Jelica and Heather break out into raucous laughter, we will turn to them and ask what's so funny. Or if Nicole and I get into a heated argument, Jelica and Heather will feel the energy and inquire if everything is all right.

We have learned that to fumble and grope is *good*. In fact, we teach sighted people how to do it. Earlier in the movement, many sighted people were learning our language, yes, but something felt off. One day Jaz, with whom I had sat with aj for our first lesson, now an esteemed fellow Protactile expert, asked me, "Do you notice how sighted people and some Deaf-Blind people who are sight-reliant always hit the mark, here and there, on the chest or head, never making a mistake?"

"Oh yes," I said. "It creeps me out too."

"Exactly. You and I, our hands often accidentally land on the wrong spot before quickly finding our way to the right location. *That* is natural!"

That was when we entered into a deeper layer of Protactile. We began teaching everyone that they need to pat their hands around. They must never allow their hands to leap straight to their destinations, for good reasons. A sighted person once accidentally poked my eye while trying to talk about how she had cried recently. "Don't do it like that," I instructed her. "You have to start here"—I guided her hand to my shoulder—"and pat, pat, pat up to where you want to go." What had once seemed our mistake has become the new perfect, and what was once their perfect has become a mistake.

IV

In the beginning, even we said it. "That's still ASL. I don't see what the big difference is supposed to be." Sure, we were doing some things differently, with the way we placed our hands to listen. Yes, there was a lot more touching. All that tapping! But the *words* themselves were the same words you find in any American Sign Language dictionary. Was Protactile really an emerging language? How about just calling it a dialect of ASL?

And there were some who wanted to keep it ASL somehow. They called it PTASL, and said that it would help those used to ASL better accept this new thing. But what had emerged continued to evolve, asserting itself, insisting on its way, its own integrity. And the words themselves began to change, too. The more we learned about our own language as it sneaked up on us, the more mixed metaphors we needed to explain it. Someone had offered that Protactile is like a car, ASL, having a new paint job. That was immediately rejected as too superficial. It's the car with a new body!

No, I had chimed in, it's more like the same body but with a new chassis and engine under it. We're still using ASL vocabulary, but how it all runs is different. Some languages do evolve that way, an old language is hot-rodded and now it's a new model!

What we all agreed on was that standard, visual ASL was no good. Only thirty percent of it is decipherable by touch. We had been following ASL by placing our hands on the speaker's hands for centuries, and there was nothing else better than it. We should have known that what we were doing was tantamount to visual lipreading, a slippery endeavor at best, impossible for most. For us ASL was indeed a sputtering jalopy, prone to breaking down in the middle of the road. We misunderstood what others were saying so often that we were experts at pretending that we understood everything.

If I told you a story about chopping down a tree in ASL and you put both of your hands over my hands, you would feel one of my hands come upright to make a tree, its finger-branches spread out, and you would feel my other hand start to chop against the forearm-trunk of the first hand. One of your hands feels the branches jolting in response. Your other hand feels the back end of the hand-axe colliding against something.

This is tactile reception of a visual construction in ASL, this one pretty robust and not hard to understand. But if there's any nuance to my story, it is lost because all you have is the basic situation of branches jolting and the back end of an axe.

What did Protactile change? The first thing was how to tell that same story. What I will do is prompt you to give me the tree. There is a specific cue, involving two taps, that means I need you to give me a hand in a certain shape, in this case a tree. With one of your hands now serving as the tree, I hold your forearm-trunk with one of my hands. Your other hand is over my other hand, now the axe. When my hand-axe starts to chop against *your* arm, you are proprioceptively receiving this message. This is no longer a merely tactile experience. What is being utilized is dynamic, "depth" perception—you *are* the tree, and you feel the axe on *both* of its sides, the back end that your hand there is following as its front edge when it collides against your arm.

It's not tactile at all. It's protactile. The dynamic, proprioceptive perception whereof I speak is the essence of the adjective "protactile." Not merely feeling something but both feeling it and feeling being felt by it. Subtle though the shift at first seemed to us, it is what has flooded us with language. It has given birth to poetry. To precision, clarity, richness, and the native inexhaustibleness of human expression. But—and it confused so many people in the beginning—the tree hand-shape I borrowed from you is the same shape as the ASL word for "tree" and the shape and motion I make with my hand-axe is the same as the ASL word for "to chop with an axe." Everything else is different, how it feels is different, but those dictionary words are the same.

For a while, saying it was like the same car body but with a new chassis and engine was the best I could do. As Protactile proclaimed itself and the more immersed we became, we noticed that new words were popping up. Some ASL words went through a convoluted etymological journey. Some ASL words were thrown out. There were Protactile words with *no* relationship whatsoever with ASL, inspired only by our own experience of the object or person or action. Protactile names became so fertile a ground that the rules that developed to govern them also began to govern elsewhere in the language. Finally, it hit me.

What we had stumbled upon was not a new chassis or engine for the old body of ASL. What we had was a *raft*. Another mode entirely, a new modality. Not even on the road! It's in the water! Water, it turns out, was the way to go.

We did have that sputtering jalopy, however. It was no good, but it was what we had. So we had rolled it onto our raft. As we cast off and began floating downstream, you can understand why many still thought we were traveling in a car. "That's still ASL," people said in the beginning. But we were all missing the most obvious truth, which was we were no longer driving on the road at all.

As we glided along, we remarked how our old car kept on jiggling forward and backward. We didn't like that. We removed the tires to make our little shelter stay in place on the raft bed. Much better!

Wriggling in and out of the car, it became a nuisance to bump into the steering wheel. So we removed that, too. Ahh, much better.

But sometimes when we stopped the raft, it lurched forward and dipped too much. We realized it was because of the weight of the engine under the hood. So there was a heave and a terrific splash. There!

We discovered that we could use the cozy space under the

hood. We unscrewed the front seats and turned them around to make it more comfortable. We began picking up sundry odds and ends along the way.

Slowly a house grew on our raft—it's going to be a houseboat! The farther along we floated, the less and less recognizable our original raft shelter became as various parts found new purposes or got thrown out in favor of new things we found or fashioned.

Around 2017, ASL speakers new to Protactile began to say, "Golly, I don't understand anything!" ASL speakers still do enjoy a head start as compared to people who know no sign language, but that advantage is dwindling. We already have people learning Protactile as their first language other than English. Many thousands of ASL words are still used, but the core vocabulary is gradually giving way to a growing Protactile vocabulary. When the new modality first emerged, we had no time to sit down and invent a million new words that were protactilely appropriate. We were busy living our lives!

The Protactile movement is such a trip I hardly ever know exactly what is happening. It feels so natural, this continuous breaking into the future, that there are often no words to describe it. From time to time, though, I pause and take stock. My reaction is always the same: Whoa! *That* is amazing. New practices, new forms, new genres, new ideas, and, always, new Protactile words. One example: I had been saying "I love you" to my family in Protactile for months before it dawned on me that I was no longer saying the ASL version of it. We'd started out by simply pressing the ASL word on each other's chests. But the Protactile inside me had rejected that word and replaced it with a much more elegant form. This word can be transliterated as "my heart on your heart."

THE VIEW
WHERE I WRITE

Vladimir Nabokov wrote standing up, scribbling on index cards while snacking on molasses. Lucille Clifton said that she wrote such short poems because that's how long she could hustle during her children's naps. Truman Capote famously described himself as a "completely horizontal author," writing longhand in bed or on a couch, with cigarettes and coffee handy. Maya Angelou often rented a room at a nearby hotel, by the month, and had the staff take out the paintings and any bric-a-brac. Charles Dickens liked changing venues but required that his traveling desk and the same ornaments be arranged just so. Agatha Christie puzzled out her murder stories in the bathtub while munching on apples. Victor Hugo abolished distractions by locking himself in a room without any clothes, for fear they would tempt him to go out. What he did permit himself was what many writers have: a view.

I am no different. Where I write, on the twenty-fifth floor

of an apartment building in downtown Saint Paul, I possess a most breathtaking view. Directly below me is a thick circular grove of—what shall I say?—soft-branched willow trees. A short distance due west lies a pond in the shape of a bear claw. I can see the reeds at its bottom and the cattails dancing around it. Due east across a field of tall grass, warm sunlight bathes a series of clumps—perhaps houses?—and a long knoll crammed with fuzzy flowers.

I never tire of tracking the snaking strip of beach that frames my vista. To the far west is a cape, to the northeast a bay, and farther east swells out a peninsula. Strangely, there are no boats. Neither are there any cars. Not as far as I am able to observe, at any rate.

My sighted friends tell me that the panorama outside my home office windows is wonderful. I smile politely. Once they've left I hurry to my desk, which faces a wall, to write and delight in the real landscape—the rug under my desk. As my fingers begin pounding away at the keys or surfing the dots of my Braille display, my feet go a-roving. The rug is unlike any other. A dear friend, the artist and philosopher Erin Manning, made it using different patterns, shapes, and fibers. She employed varying thicknesses and lengths, ranging from tall tufts to the untufted woven base of the rug.

A topological marvel, the rug's outline is map-like and the intentional hole is a revelation. My right heel often nestles in the circular grove, while any number of my left toes may be taking a dip in the hole. The rug is the beginning of a new world. We in the Protactile movement have been laying foundations dealing with the most basic human requirements—language, co-presence, space, navigation, and even art—but little did I know how much decoration could offer.

So much out there in the world, and here in my home, is tactilely monotonous. Floors, walls, surfaces—all tyrannies of uniform texture. It turns out that our mental health demands forests, mountains, valleys, flowers, animals, waterfalls, and crashing waves! Be it a rug that's also a work of art or cheapo freebie swag galore, we need to populate our environments. We need a mess, a storm, a cacophony.

I regret to say that I am, deep down, a selfish man. I won't share my view! But even deeper down burns my love for our future. Thankfully, Erin made *two* rugs for me. The other, bigger, even more specular view hangs on a wall, to receive our hands or shoulders or cheeks or noses or lips as we pass by or, frequently, stop. It is easy to take down should friends desire to have our feet discover its wonders while we converse, or to drape it over our laps for us to gaze upon it together, whispering and exclaiming, with our hands.

METATACTILE
KNOWLEDGE

"How did you know?"

That's a response I often get when I interact with people. How did I know that their shoulder needed a massage, or that they were hungry or sad, or a spot on their arm was itchy? The owners of pets I meet are also amazed. Almost immediately I've found their pets' sweet spots. "That's right! She loves that. But how did you know?"

On one of our first dates, my future wife asked, "How did you know?" Without realizing what I was doing, I had pressed her Melt Button. (She wishes me to inform my readers, lest your imagination run away, that it was nothing naughty.)

When our twin sons were born prematurely (now a happily meaningless fact), the nurses in the NICU were impressed by what I did. I felt right away that my sons' skins were too sensitive to stroke. I just held them or squeezed their arms and legs, even firmly, but I knew not to stroke.

The nurses were going to give instructions to that effect, but there was no need.

I wasn't conscious of it. It was natural. So natural, in fact, that I didn't have a name for it, this skill that goes beyond just feeling texture, heft, shape, and temperature. I'd like to call it metatactile knowledge. It involves feeling being felt, being able to read people like open Braille books, and seeing through our hands and the antennae of and within our bodies. It involves many senses, senses that we all have but are almost never mentioned— the axial, locomotive, kinesthetic, vestibular . . . all "tactile" to some extent, but going beyond "touch."

I did write about it in passing. I even wrote one poem that's all about it, without realizing what I was documenting. Here's "Clamor":

> All things living and dead cry out to me
> when I touch them. The dog, gasping for air,
> is drowning in ecstasy, its neck shouting
> Dig in, dig in. Slam me, slam me,
> demands one door while another asks to remain
> open. My wife again asks me
> how did I know just where and how
> to caress her. I can be too eager to listen:
> The scar here on my thumb is a gift
> from a cracked bowl that begged to be broken.

As my little ode to metatactile knowledge attests, it extends to interactions with objects. I know, I know, objects are dead and have no feelings. But they still respond to tactile contact and actions. Their design and the materials with which they are made do draw people to handle them in certain ways. Indeed, product developers study this all the time.

But there are quirks, unpredictable things that we do or discover. Take the little subscription-form inserts inside magazines: One of my earliest memories is of tearing such subscription forms into handfuls of soft, fuzzy confetti. The paper those are printed on is pulpy and so rippable! Other kinds of paper do not have the same delicious give, but they may be perfect for folding into airplanes—their lines so crisp and taut!

Probably most people can relate a little to what I'm talking about when they think of bubble wrap. Do not those rows of little tight buns clamor, as it were, to be popped? Another example that should be familiar: Reese's peanut-butter cups. Remember those old TV commercials where kids played with a cup, pushing out the center and leaving a hole in the middle? Think on it. There is nothing visual to suggest how one might play with these cups in this way. Tactile investigation is what uncovers the fact that the center is softer than the rim of solid chocolate.

So this is nothing new. It's an element of human life. Yet, as Lyle Crist asks in his fine 1974 biography of Richard Kinney, a DeafBlind poet and true explorer of the world:

> How much do we *enjoy* what is around us? How many really understand the melody inherent in—what shall we use?—the Golden Gate Bridge? How many ever get out of the car, feel the bridge moving gently in the wind swells, how many of us put our hands out to touch the cables, feel the bridge sing to us?

I inhabit it all the time and apply metatactile knowledge to all my interactions with people, things, the world, and myself. I have Reese's "fun things to do" for a thousand things. A thousand other things sing to me. Of course, when I play King

Kong and crush an empty water bottle or when I snap off the cotton ends of a Q-tip in order to unroll the stem and fold it into a flower, it's more about me than the object. The point is that we all are in continuous conversation.

Except that not everyone is as engaged in conversation as we could be. As a second-generation DeafBlind person, I took it for granted that most DeafBlind people knew and interacted with the world as I did, through an abundance of touch. After all, we don't have the same visual and auditory distractions that hearing-sighted people have, distractions that leave their tactile skills in a neglected, dormant state. Of course touch is everything to us!

When I began my work as a Braille instructor and a Pro-tactile trainer, however, I came to observe things that weren't always apparent in social settings. One of the first things I noticed in my Braille sessions was how poorly my students figured out their surroundings. Or else they waited to be told where things were, to be guided, as if they could move about in spaces only preapproved by others for our use. Many also had trouble locating things on a page of Braille. Yes, it takes practice to be able to read those tiny dots, but there are broader details—such as where paragraphs start and end or which way is up or down—that I thought wouldn't be elusive.

I found out more about this troubling pattern during Pro-tactile trainings. Random example: A man came up to me during a snack break, asking for help opening his bag of potato chips. I was puzzled, and learned that what he always did, or tried to do, was to take hold of two sides and pull them apart. I inquired if he was aware of the hole along one of the seams, placed there expressly to help open the bag. He was awestruck. In his years buying chips and other snacks, he never knew about the little holes or tears in the seams provided by the manufacturers. "Who told you about this?" he demanded. No one had. I just picked it up and have always "known" about this feature.

What the man had was a bad case of tactile freeze. Isabell Florence, a fellow Protactile trainer, explains, "Tactile freeze is learned. It is natural for us to explore everything tactilely. But when I was a kid, they hit my hands for touching."

I hope there is less hand-slapping going on these days, but DeafBlind children are surrounded by hearing-sighted people—their parents, teachers, peers, and the horribly but uncannily titled "interveners," their constant adult companions-interpreters-teacher's-aides-guides—whose visual biases and values serve to mentally, socially, and emotionally slap our hands. Everyone in DeafBlind education pays lip service to touch, but they don't really know what to do with it. They do arbitrary things that are jarring, swooping in to pat or present an object only to step back and, some time later, make another contact, this time to rub a shoulder.

What of those among us who become DeafBlind as adults and didn't have their hands slapped as children? When we start to become deaf or blind, our first contacts are doctors, who try to save or fix our sight and hearing. Next, we get into vocational rehabilitation, whose agencies often have policies that insist on touch-related things being the last resort. It is also a field that has almost no professionals or instructors who are themselves DeafBlind. Most of us are left to figure out tactile communication on our own. Because programs that are supposed to serve us almost never hire DeafBlind people to teach us what we need to know, it often takes a long time before we enter the DeafBlind community.

And there's our society, which is extremely anti-tactile, Reese's peanut-butter cups notwithstanding: Do Not Touch. So many things are buried in tactilely blank boxes and packages. Vital information is printed on flat surfaces. Many businesses prohibit any contact between their employees and customers. Police recite the mantra that "hands kill." Things of great tactile import and beauty are kept behind glass. Knobs, switches, handles, levers, keys, and buttons are giving way to things called, strange to say, "touch screens."

Fortunately, there are some who have escaped such oppression with our tactile fields relatively intact. One is a young man named Ben Reid, who is currently attending my alma mater, Minnesota State Academy for the Deaf. I first met him five years ago when he was eleven and his family visited Minnesota to check out what it had to offer. The instant he came into the room, he found me and sized me up. He also found the small latch on my Braille display and opened it to examine the device. There was a quick, wordless exchange in flutters and pressures that, if translated into words, would run something like this: "Careful with that latch." "Yeah, it could easily break." "Okay, you know what you're doing." "Thanks. This is really cool!" Then his first words: "Is it expensive?" As I gave his family a tour of the skyways in downtown Saint Paul, I smiled and smiled because Ben was all over the place. His orbit of exploration was huge and all-encompassing. I'm very glad to report that it still is.

It doesn't surprise me that the young man's mother is also DeafBlind. Christy Reid understands that touching is seeing. She bristles whenever sighted people attempt to restrain her. "Often when I reach out and start exploring," she says, "people will say something that makes me feel foolish, and I explain, 'I'm just looking and I need to touch it.' I hate it when they try to stop me from touching."

This is one of the things the Protactile revolution is

addressing, this awful way we are conditioned to yield to visual culture at our expense. As much of my tactilehood as I've enjoyed, I still catch myself holding back for something as stupid as appearance—appearance within a visual context entirely outside of my reach. Take a line of people in an eatery. Most DeafBlind people will try to follow the line, be cooperative, all the while trying not to touch anyone. It takes conscious effort to establish new habits, such as cutting in front of a line if the setup isn't accessible, firmly reaching out and establishing contact and some tactile-gestural communication with a person in front of me, or bypassing an impractical counter to go directly to the person I need to communicate with about my order. Also, when shopping with an access assistant, it used to be that they pulled me back at times in order to prevent my touching a stranger. It took some doing, but I've retrained my assistants to allow, even help, me establish contact with anyone near me or near the things I want to grab off a shelf. Indeed, establishing such contact has made my tasks go smoother, since I can tactilely tell someone she doesn't need to move away, that I just want this item. It saves a lot of time, too—no more wasteful waiting for someone to move when what I want isn't even directly in front of her.

In addition to the practical benefits of establishing tactile contact as much as possible, there is something more primal at stake. Sighted people take this for granted, and may not appreciate how important this is, but every day when they go out they receive acknowledgment of their existence in the form of smiles, waves, nods, murmured greetings. Where is my share in this reassurance that we are here?

These experiences and thoughts made me appreciate why many sighted Deaf people in the old days refrained from speaking ASL in public. They instinctively felt that ASL did not belong in open society, and imagined that their moving hands would startle, offend. They also took all responsibility for communication, either attempting speech and lip-reading or carrying a notepad wherever they went.

Then something happened. Deaf people began to impose visual culture wherever they went, forcing hearing people to make eye contact and to gesture back. They spoke ASL freely in public and thought nothing of breaking mainstream rules. They thought nothing of staying in a restaurant hours after ending their meals, much to the consternation of the owners, occupying tables like that. Occupying space, transforming it into Deaf space. The Deaf Pride movement was what happened. My parents' generation was the first to not carry a notepad. It was now hearing people's responsibility to look for paper and a pen. Older notepad-carrying Deaf folks pointed out that it was faster to have a notepad ready, but my parents and their contemporaries couldn't be bothered with it. It was a different world.

And now the world is undergoing another change. Whereas touch was once forbidden and accidental, now, for a growing number of people, it is a right. Yes, it startles. It may offend. But in my efforts to exercise and expand my tactilehood by seeking people out and touching them purposefully, I have found that sighted people can handle it. Metatactile knowledge resides in all of us, and it surges forward to meet others, to respond in kind. Some strangers I encounter are so responsive I marvel, "How did they know? That's exactly it!"

One truth that has been impressed upon me is that one can know only so much without being known. We've hidden ourselves for too long, our hands tucked away, letting the world go by. No more. It's time we introduced ourselves and got to know you.

PART TWO

FOREVER AND FLUENTLY FUMBLING

DISTANTISM

It is with a wry shake of my head on your arm that I find myself introducing a fancy new word. As a poet I dislike jargon. But sometimes we do need a new word, and it can change the way we see everything. That's what happened to the sighted Deaf community with "audism." Although it was first coined in 1975, by the Deaf scholar Tom L. Humphries, it didn't receive a full discussion until after the hearing-sighted linguist Harlan Lane used it in his 1993 book *The Mask of Benevolence: Disabling the Deaf Community*. Sighted Deaf people had always known that hearing society discriminated on the basis of hearing status and oral speech ability, but the new word suddenly made it much easier to identify and analyze.

As is typical of our community, several DeafBlind folks proposed variations on the Deaf theme. But none of them caught on. More recently, however, "vidism," referring to the worship and validation of sight supremacy, has gained some traction. It's a helpful concept for two reasons. First, it places a finger on some of the ways sighted Deaf communities replicate their own oppression by oppressing us. The second reason is that the hearing blind community did not yet have a term to describe sighted privilege and bias, other than the generic "ableism," until "ocularcentricism" found an awkward entry in academia. Our brother Bryen Yunashko has done much to define and address vidism.

Yet addressing both audism and vidism still leaves too much behind glass. I knew there was something bigger there, and I longed for something to shatter that pane of mystification. Something to allow me to wrap my hands around its throat and say, "I've found you out, you old serpent!"

The sense of that malaise that affects all of us, DeafBlind and non-DeafBlind alike, had been growing stronger and stronger ever since the Protactile movement started in 2007. It has taught us so much about who we are. About what is natural and true. About how to live. About language. What we once put up with we could no longer tolerate.

What, I wondered, is the opposite of tactile? Researching our community's history, I see that we have always been tactile. But hearing and sighted people have always sought to keep our tactilehoods in check. We've always been denied access to some of the most basic human rights. What should we call this force of oppression?

A STANDING APART

I propose to call it distantism. The English word "distance" comes from "distantia," Latin for "a standing apart." "Distantism" refers to the privileging of the distance senses of hearing and vision. The ways in which many cultures have evolved on the almost exclusive basis of these two senses have indeed been harmful to us. That insistence on sight or hearing to function in society means only one thing for us: death.

But that's putting it too simplistically. Each form of social bigotry has its distinctive personality and its unique set of intertwining evils. So I will dwell on the concept of distantia, or a standing apart, which lies at the heart of distantism. We already have a Protactile word that describes people who pull away from touch, who refuse to connect. It is an attitude and a behavior. Many hearing and sighted societies prize it highly, and their members seek to maintain physical distance, however thin those margins may be. Their rulers and heroes stand alone—the more remote they are, the more highly esteemed they are. The less privileged are squeezed closer together due to poverty or exploitation, or as punishment, and distantism manifests itself in restricting or constraining their living conditions and, above all, removing them out of sight and hearing. For all the hype around its ability to connect the world, technology has often served to isolate people in every other way.

Are sighted and hearing people wrong to use their distance senses and let it affect how they live? No. If they wish to be all protuberant eyeballs and flapping ears, they are welcome to such an existence. But we have problems when they impose their distantism on us.

Let's read a classic distantist statement, found in the preface to a textbook for teaching DeafBlind people how to use a white cane:

> The loss of both sight and hearing constitutes one of the severest disabilities known to human beings. Essentially, it deprives an individual of the two primary senses through which we acquire awareness of and information about the world around us, and it drastically limits effective

communication and freedom of movement, which are necessary for full and active participation in society.

It used to be impossible to argue with a statement like that. Now, with a critique of distantism we can begin to break it down. It's an old trick, blaming injustice on its targets so that the privileged can pretend there's nothing wrong. We are at the bottom of society because, what? Because we are Deaf-Blind. Which cannot be helped. Therefore, we belong at the bottom of society. It's an amazingly easy trick to pull. They take things out of our reach and then they say we have limited awareness. Whatever they do is our fault.

I wish I could share everything this critique has unearthed for me, but it would take years to write! For now, I will touch on a few things that I think tell us a great deal about how distantism works in our lives as DeafBlind people.

INTERVENORS

Despite the many barriers we encounter in society, we can gain much awareness about the world around us. But when we go exploring or when we just exist, sighted and hearing people rush in to intervene. Can they help us? Please don't touch. They will be happy to describe it to us. They will guide us. No, they will get it for us. It's much easier that way. Hello! My name is Katie and I'm your Intervenor!

One of the things I have pondered is why, very early in the history of education of DeafBlind children, school administrators started assigning each one of us a special teacher-companion. This wasn't always the case. In some classes we shared a teacher in common and we had each other. We can see in the record how distantism set in, and how hearing and sighted people wanted things to look right. It didn't look good when we went around "groping in the dark." It didn't look good for us to cluster together and have too much fun. Education meant we had to sit behind a desk.

The solution was to assign each one of us a sighted companion. Such teachers made it possible for us to sit apart and for the classroom teacher to stand in front of us. They made us hearing and sighted by proxy. Even though we were in constant contact with our special teachers, the pair of us made for a tidy unit that could and did stand apart. It also made for a most inspiring sight, the self-sacrificing teacher laboring as our only link to the world. It's not a miracle unless there's a miracle worker.

Today those special companions are called Intervenors or Interveners. The title is altogether too apt. Intervenors who eavesdrop on this article will protest, "But I let Jimmy touch anything he wants to!" My friend, no. It's not just a matter of letting or encouraging. There's a whole cultural element involved. There are distantist modes of touch and there are protactile modes of touch. Many cultures mediate physical contact in different ways, such as some using handshakes in greetings while others favor the kissing of cheeks, but those instances are exceptions to and governed by distantist rules. A protactile grounding, a whole field of relations built on touch, means that a handshake or a kiss is not in contrast to distantism but part of a larger lexicon of touch. A distantist cannot truly teach or empower our children to live and learn as protactile people. Yet the field of education of DeafBlind children has never included us as teachers. Why is that?

THE ROAD NOT TAKEN

September 30, 1841, might have been the beginning of a wonderful alternative history. On that day, our brother Oliver Caswell, an eleven-year-old DeafBlind boy, entered the Perkins Institution, where our sister Laura Bridgman, the DeafBlind girl who Charles Dickens and others had made world-famous as an educational marvel, had already been a student for four years. Amid the mass of new people he met on that day, Laura was the one who immediately interested him, and they latched together. Observing this, Samuel Gridley Howe, the school's director, decided to enlist Laura as his "auxiliary" during Oliver's first lessons. They proceeded with finger spelling, skipping the more laborious and counterproductive steps with which Howe had initiated Laura's lessons. Thereafter Laura eagerly continued to teach Oliver, devoting many hours each week to the enterprise. One of Perkins's most prized possessions is a portrait of Laura teaching Oliver to read and write. Fortune also hugged them when Howe embarked on a long honeymoon in Europe.

In Deaf education, Deaf teachers were involved from Day One. Many graduates were promptly hired as teachers, and Deaf teachers went on to found schools all over the world. Blind graduates of early schools for the blind also were hired as teachers and continue to play a leading role in that field. But in the education of DeafBlind children, we have not seen the same pattern. There are thousands of Intervenors working today. There are hundreds of teachers who work with our children in Deaf, blind, and public schools. There are hundreds of early-intervention specialists. None of those professionals are themselves DeafBlind. What happened to cause so complete a shutout of tactile teachers and role models?

When Howe returned to his post at Perkins, he found that Laura had mingled too much with teachers and fellow students. She had learned too much about religion and had many questions. He claimed that his experiment had been ruined. He had wanted to find out if Laura would think of or discover God without anyone mentioning God or religion to her. He made some radical changes, and, later, for a period of five years Laura was in the company of one single teacher. Any suggestions of a future in a widening social circle were abandoned. Perkins set an example for the world, still in effect today, of assigning each one of us a special teacher-companion. They were to help us, keep us safe, protect us from bad influences, and, we can now see, make sure we aspire to the distantist ideal. We learned to wait to be told things and not to find out things for ourselves.

It is a common expectation and outcome of some forms of oppression that their targets must fit in a narrow space of cooperation and gratitude. The idea with distantism is that we can never uphold it perfectly, but we should make a continuous failed attempt to do so. This continuous failed attempt reassures society that we agree with their values. We are to be good, but never good enough. The field, which Howe firmly sent on its current course, excludes us because it needs to maintain a certain level of failure. If its goal were to succeed in educating us, it would have long ago embraced the tactile worlds we manifest and would have valued us as teachers and leaders. Instead, distantism is the first condition, and for that to make sense, the field needs its work to be difficult and expensive, not easy and effective.

UNDER DIFFERENT NAMES

We adults also receive intervention that serves a similar function. In the United States we have Support Service Providers, and in the United Kingdom they are called Communicator Guides. In Canada, they don't bother to pretend it's something different. Their Intervenors serve children and adults alike.

I am not saying that we don't need sighted assistants. After all, we do live in a distantist society, and we should avail ourselves of distance-information readers. However, the way our SSP services are performed can be smothering. That's why a key concern of the Protactile movement is autonomy. When I teach Protactile, I like to make it easier to remember what it means and how to spell it by breaking it down into three parts:

AUTO: They do a lot of things automatically, taking over, making decisions for us, making assumptions.

NO: We need to say "No!" to such automatic actions.

MY: We need to say "My!"—we will do things our way and make our own decisions.

Sometimes I get a new SSP and she asks for my shopping list. She is ready to take charge and have me merely holding on to the cart. She's confused when I do not give her a list and I take charge, directing us toward the places where we will find what I want. It is my responsibility to learn and know the world around me. It is part of her job to help me update that knowledge as we go along, but it is not her job to retain any of this knowledge herself.

Having an SSP is still useful, but it makes such an enormous difference how it's done and when. Sadly, most SSP, CG, and Intervenor programs leave the professionals' distantism intact. As a result, they often take charge, make assumptions, push our canes away from making contact, pull us back from people, put themselves in the middle of interactions instead of supporting our direct communication with others, and guide us in such a way as to maintain a margin between us and the world around us. No wonder we have limited awareness!

Their distantism finds its ugliest though unconscious expression at many of our own gatherings, conferences, and retreats. The routine is always the same: We are each assigned an SSP. Instead of helping us connect with each other, they end up being the ones with whom we talk the most. Their presence creates a network of distantism that separates us from each other or makes it harder for us to find each other. They also can destroy moments when we cluster and go tactile. A friend shared with me an experience he had with a yoga activity at a popular retreat catering to our community. The yoga instructor was a sister, and she wanted the group to do it in Protactile style. So there was a happy clustering, and people helped each other and passed on information. But it didn't look right, and one of the SSPs standing back intervened by going to her "client" to correct his position. "That's not what the position is, it is this." Soon the other SSPs slipped into the group. In a few moments there was a nice straight row, everyone paired off and standing apart.

THE WHITE CANE

Even when we shake off those pesky intervenors, distantism follows us still in the form of the white cane. Now, I love my cane, but it was also one of the first things that told me there is something wrong. What this means for our present discussion is that the instant we feel the need for a cane, we are in distantist territory. One of our long-term goals should be to claim more and more territory where we abandon our canes because the design of these environments is tactilely accessible and appropriate.

For going out in public, I think we still need to ask the question: Why were we given the white cane? The three words Orientation and Mobility specialists repeat like a mantra are "independence," "freedom," and "safety." Our brother Robert Sirvage has noted that in American Sign Language all three are said the same way. Our crossed wrists turn away from each other, moving apart, as if breaking out of handcuffs. That's freedom, and also independence and safety. I now realize that such notions are the ultimate distantist fantasy. Our being in a bubble of two people, an intervenor guiding it and speaking for us and explaining the world to us, is only second best. What is most desirable is for us to be in a bubble alone.

The white cane makes it possible for us to go many places over a wide variety of terrain, all the while avoiding contact with our environment except through our cane. It is a magic wand that conjures up a bubble for us to float in. Sighted Orientation and Mobility instructors have always taught us one-on-one, the better to dance circles around us and make sure the skin of the bubble thickens. They like to scout out a location first, find a path through it, and then bring us there, saying, "Go straight until you feel a curb, then take a forty-five-degree turn and walk until you encounter a railing." A code of aimed turns and sailing until we hit something, then another turn.

The field of education has yet to accept any DeafBlind instructors, adamant in the belief that we cannot teach each other to travel. They are right—we cannot possibly teach each other how to travel in their sterile, desolate, meaningless mode where the goal is for us to go down the middle, in a straight line. They want us to disturb the world as little as possible. Ironically, sighted people make that easy to accomplish by parting like the Red Sea before our rod. Joke: How am I supposed to find anyone if everyone runs away from me?

The bubbles they put us in are sometimes so thick they are more like tanks. I cannot count the times I have approached a DeafBlind friend and had the feeling I've just interrupted their process of steaming forward. Often they're holding something in their other hand, and I must wait for them to disassemble their tank-bubble before we can interact. That's why I have worked on making my bubble as thin as possible, ready to pop the instant there's an opportunity for connection. For me, this has meant finding the right cane: a slender beauty made of fiberglass. It's so light that I can hold it like a pencil if I want to, with just two fingers. It's no tank. It's a mere whisker, sometimes feeling ahead, sometimes tucked in my armpit and dragging behind me, allowing my hands to explore.

One of the modes of travel I love is co-navigation, traveling with another, especially a fellow DeafBlind person. I agree with Robert's suggestion that we need community-based approaches. This goes against the whole thrust of the rehabilitation system, which is a monument to distantism. It's built on one-on-one instruction, which effectively isolates us and tells us that we are broken and need to be fixed.

FINAL IRONY

Before I bring up one more thing about distantism, let's read that quote again:

> The loss of both sight and hearing constitutes one of the severest disabilities known to human beings. Essentially, it deprives an individual of the two primary senses through which we acquire awareness of and information about the world around us, and it drastically limits effective communication and freedom of movement, which are necessary for full and active participation in society.

The final irony is that a DeafBlind man, the late Robert J. Smithdas, wrote these words. Many hearing and sighted people have expressed the same sentiments, but distantism is so pervasive that we all have internalized it. Helen Keller thought of us as being imprisoned in the "double dungeon of darkness and silence" and described us as "the loneliest people on Earth." She was being fanciful, but what is true is that the marginalization we experience is too often literal, involving physical margins.

That we find distantism even in ourselves is good news, for it proves that it is a serious, society-wide sickness. When our sisters, the magnificent Jelica Nuccio and aj granda, launched the Protactile movement, we knew it was a historic event. Now that we know more about distantism and how poisonous it is, their achievement seems all the more astonishing.

Think about it. Billions of people on this planet, and all of them agreeing that hearing and vision are required for leading full, normal lives. Billions of people of one mind that being

DeafBlind must be an unendurable fate. Billions of dollars poured into the hope of medical cures. Distantism, that old serpent, held the whole world in its remote-control spell.

And then our sisters from Seattle had the audacity to say that there's a DeafBlind way. To say that hearing and vision are not necessary. To say that the only cure we need is each other. Can you feel the world shaking as it starts to, finally, come together?

DEAFBLIND:
A BRIEF HISTORY OF
OUR NAME

It is six degrees below zero here in Hopkins, Minnesota. Ten inches of snow are on the ground. My cheeks are burning. This morning's *Christian Science Monitor* delivered a slap in our faces. For months, my colleagues in the Protactile movement and I had corresponded with one of their journalists, and we had invited him to join us for a week of curriculum development meetings in Oregon, where he did some filming and interviews. And now the video story about our rapidly evolving language has gone live.

The text of the story, as well as the transcript of the video, referred to us as "deaf-blind." That set off a firestorm. We had always identified ourselves as DeafBlind, and at no point during our engagement with the journalist did we ever say or write "deaf-blind." The journalist explained to me that the staff editors had changed "DeafBlind" because the style guide from the National Center on Disability and Journalism recommends "deaf-blind."

In the ensuing back-and-forth with the editors, I found myself slipping into the familiar position of explaining our name. The editors tried to make it an issue of nomenclature. They also asked for documentation. I kept shifting the issue back to that of respect. They had disregarded how we identify ourselves. All they needed to do was extend the courtesy of following how we prefer to be called.

Because we shouldn't have to defend our position or supply documentation, I hesitate to write this essay. The issue should always be that of common courtesy. But since we inevitably end up doing some explaining, it may be helpful to provide an account of how we came to insist on being identified as Deaf-Blind. It would certainly save time when something like this happens again, although our goal should always be to obtain unconditional respect.

All right. In the nineteenth century, we had a pungent pot-pourri of labels sprinkled over our heads, including Blind Deaf-Mute and Deaf, Dumb, and Blind! Yes, exclamation points often attended. Notice how there are three things mentioned. This reflected the Victorian understanding of muteness—by which they meant not speaking orally—as a distinct disability. Many of us were considered as suffering under not two but three afflictions. Thomas Arnold, a British educator, termed it "a fearful trio of calamities."

Then dumbness began to lose its status as a cornerstone disability. Alexander Graham Bell and other oralists insisted that Deaf people could be and should be taught to speak orally and to read lips. As part of their propaganda machine, they campaigned for the removal of "Dumb" and "Mute" from the names of schools, organizations, and publications. The reality of deafness they could not deny, but dumbness was a figment, a phantom, a demon to be exorcised by steampunk Science. They imagined a very near future where all Deaf people spoke English perfectly, could read lips a mile away, and would marry only healthy hearing people so as to milk the "deaf variety of the human race" out of existence. Bell did accept, however, that DeafBlind people could not be expected to get on with the program, while sighted Deaf people had no excuse.

Some Deaf people resisted by emphasizing that they were indeed mute. They began to use the word "silent" as a subversive concept. The National Association of the Deaf, for example, named its official organ *The Silent Worker*. Others who did speak orally as well as American Sign Language, rather than going with "deaf," labeled themselves "semi-mute."

But by the early decades of the twentieth century, this particular aspect of oralist ideology was so pervasive that even the National Association of the Deaf voted to condemn "mute" and "dumb" terminology. From that point on, it was just "deaf." One effect of that development was that we no longer carried a combination of three possible labels. It was down to two. It was either blind-deaf or deaf-blind. William Wade, a steel industrialist from Pittsburgh who first became interested in us after meeting nine-year-old Helen Keller and giving her two dogs, published a monograph in 1901 called *The Deaf-Blind* and followed it up in 1904 with *The Blind-Deaf.* He traveled across the United States and Canada to meet over a hundred DeafBlind people, gifting Hall Braillewriters, customized items, and stipends and inviting many to vacation at his estate in Oakmont, Pennsylvania. In the summer of 1901, he underwrote a historic gathering of DeafBlind students and adults in Buffalo, to take part in the meeting of the Convention of American Instructors of the Deaf and to enjoy the Pan-American Exposition.

Of the two terms, "deaf-blind" became the standard and remained thus for most of the twentieth century. During the 1960s, however, strange things started to happen to the definition of "deaf-blind." The rubella epidemic saw an explosion in the number of "multiply handicapped" babies being born, including DeafBlind children with or without other disabilities. In the 1970s, there were mandates and much money for "mainstreaming" those children in public schools. Hearing and sighted educators stuffed as many children as possible under the "deaf-blind" classification.

Historically, unlike for Deaf communities and blind communities in education, we have never been enlisted to serve as teachers of DeafBlind children. As the ranks of hearing and sighted teachers swelled in response to the rubella epidemic and a growing list of etiologies, the practice of excluding our community continued. The lack of our involvement allowed them to apply the label "deaf-blind" to a vast number of children with multiple other disabilities, while always insisting that "deafblindness" be considered the primary disability. In fact, the stuffing strategy gave them yet another excuse for our exclusion. "Keep in mind," I was repeatedly told by educators when I pushed for the hiring of DeafBlind teachers, "that most of the students are severely and profoundly disabled and not like you." Never mind that any child would benefit from having a DeafBlind teacher.

Then a tiny tweak took place in Europe. Hearing and sighted professionals, especially those who worked for charities, felt that "deaf-blind" no longer reflected those children's plight. They began eliminating the hyphen to make it a single word. As Salvatore Lagati of Italy's Servizio di Consulenza Pedagogica explained in a 1993 paper, "deafblindness is a condition presenting other difficulties than those caused by deafness and blindness." Rather than it being deafness and blindness added together, their logic went, it was deafness and blindness multiplied. Dropping the hyphen proved useful in their fund-raising efforts, giving them infinite occasion to explain how "deafblindness" is much more—read: worse—than the sum of the two parts.

As charities the world over scrambled to remove the hyphen, it became clear that similar groups in the United States were declining the upgrade. One reason was that our DeafBlind organizations rejected the uniqueness rhetoric. Although we were never directly involved in the education of DeafBlind children, our organizations at least had a say in nomenclature debates. We preferred to think of our lot as being simply deaf and blind, nothing worse. The shrug was in keeping with our traditional stance as a community of identity rather than that of culture.

But even that stance was shifting. Starting in the 1960s, we gathered in person with increasing frequency. In 1973, inspired by those social opportunities, a Black DeafBlind woman from Cleveland named Doris Callahan ran for president of the National Association of the Deaf-Blind—today the American Association of the DeafBlind—on a plan to host annual national conventions. After her election, this idea was put into motion, and the first convention took place in Cleveland in 1975. Other major gatherings followed, including retreats, camps, expos, and cruises.

Attendees of the seventh annual AADB convention in August 1982 raved about their time on the University of

Northern Colorado campus. It was the first time, according to longtime AADB president Roderick Macdonald's history of the organization, that "all participants were housed in the same building, which was also the location for all meetings and all meals, making it possible for many deaf-blind people to come and go from their rooms, their meals and their meetings without assistance." By 1989, Roderick would present on the possibility of a DeafBlind culture. His paper "Deaf-blindness: An Emerging Culture?" was delivered during the Deaf Way international conference, and he speculated that

> if deaf-blind people were allowed more opportunities to interact with each other on a continuous basis, they would gradually develop a tactile, manual language ideally suited to their needs—that is, to the sense of touch. While this tactile language would have its roots in spoken and signed languages, it would gradually develop the unique grammar and syntax typical of independent languages.

Twenty years later, his augury was more than fulfilled with the emergence of Protactile, our first independent language. At the time he presented his arguments, though, it was easy to mistake them as an extrapolation of Deaf cultural discourse. Indeed, our community included those who grew up in the Deaf sighted world. They had made a great invasion of our community during the 1970s, when many of them learned that they had Usher syndrome and were becoming progressively blind. My father was one of them, but thankfully he ignored the warnings not to have children and pass down the genetic calamity. As his generation of people with Usher syndrome came into our community, they caused some confusion. For example, "Bill," after losing his job and his status in a Deaf community when he became increasingly blind, would start attending our events. He would say that "Tom" wasn't "culturally deaf-blind" because he didn't speak ASL. Rather, Bill would embrace "Mary" as a fellow "culturally deaf-blind" person because she graduated from a Deaf school and spoke ASL fluently. Here Bill obviously had much yet to learn, because Tom used a cane, read Braille, and communicated tactilely, whereas Mary was still in denial, refusing to use a cane or learn Braille. It would take time before Bill would appreciate that if anyone were to be considered culturally deaf-blind, it would be Tom and not Mary.

Not all Deaf cultural values had to be shorn away. One value that did help to rewrite our community DNA was the expectation that we have a common and natural language of our own and, through that language, build our own physical spaces. At first, many newcomers from the Deaf community tried to make ASL and visual spaces be those things for our community. That never worked, but the desire to be able to communicate through a native language did lead to Protactile. Ironically, many of the same people who brought in this desire were the most resistant to Protactile, because for them ASL still represented that desire.

When sighted Deaf communities started to capitalize "deaf" to denote a cultural identity, some people in our community immediately wanted to capitalize "deaf-blind." In this they were being too Deaf-minded. The idea of capitalization needed to be more finely filtered through our collective thought. In 1993, a town hall meeting was held in the basement of a church in Minneapolis. My father, who was then serving on the board of our local organization, had convened it to consider the question of nomenclature. I was fourteen years old. I can still feel the excitement in the room as everyone spoke their mind. What resulted was not only the capitalization of the "deaf" part—which would have been copying Textbook Deaf Culture—but also the capitalization of the "blind" part. Members with no background in the Deaf world supported capitalization and were emphatic that both parts be capitalized.

That was not all. The assembled body also decided to do away with the hyphen. The peculiar spelling was adopted, and our organization's name changed to Minnesota DeafBlind Association, thus sparking a trend that continues to this writing. Today "DeafBlind" is one of the only things that enjoys widespread consensus among diverse demographics and factions within our community. Mortal enemies over other matters, including the controversial Protactile movement, are in agreement that DeafBlind is our name.

Some people have and will continue to misread it. By capitalizing it, are we establishing that ours is a cultural identity? Yes, but not because we have a textbook version of it. By removing the hyphen, are we stressing that it's not deaf plus blind but something more? Yes, but not because "more" means "worse."

Our compound, doubly capitalized name, coined before the Internet popularized such spellings, is admittedly an awkward one. At nine letters long it is unwieldly, and we often go with "DB" for short. We've had to fight for its recognition and our own definition of it. Maybe it's even meant to be slightly off-putting, like it's saying, "It may be weird, but it's us. Deal with it." As such, it serves as a good test because we have so much more than just our name that demands respect and support.

It is now a sunny morning six days later. The snow has melted some. My cheeks are bristly-soft with a beard I've let grow since last Thursday. In my inbox is a message from Mark

Sappenfield, editor of the *Christian Science Monitor*. "After a discussion among the staff," it says, "we have decided to change our style to DeafBlind as a default, but also to ask those interviewed how they would like to be identified and to respect those wishes." There's more, of course. What we expose affects everyone else. Sappenfield continues, "It is . . . abundantly clear that the old model of journalists being the gatekeepers . . . is all but past; we are now partners with the communities we cover. What I learned in this experience is that it goes not only for our content, but for how we let our readers talk through our pages. We need to be more flexible and fluid to honor their voices."

CO-NAVIGATION

I

In 1996, my father—Lee Clark, a DeafBlind community leader and educator based in Minnesota—and a hearing-sighted colleague of his, Linda Hanke, were invited to present at a conference in Vancouver, British Columbia. Dad decided to take all of us there and make a little vacation out of the trip. I was in high school and it was my first international flight. The majority of the attendees were dewy-eyed college students studying to be "Intervenors." The Canadian presenters spoke incessantly of the value of "intervention," a word that baffled me. When it came up for what seemed the thousandth time, I nudged Linda and asked what it meant. Her explanation stunned me. "Intervention," she said, crinkling her nose at the term, "is where you interrupt, step in, take over. In order to fix something or prevent a bad thing from happening."

"Do you mean," I asked in mock wonderment, "we Deaf-Blind people are the bad thing that's going to happen?"

"That's the idea," she said. We both laughed. We were assured that we had it much better in the United States, where, instead of Intervenors, we had Support Service Providers. I remember sitting back with a sense of satisfaction. Our feeling of superiority, however, was not at all warranted. Yet the concept of "intervention"—the sighted leading the blind—did and does deserve our scorn.

At the time of the conference, the most recent published definition, from the Fall 1995 issue of *Deaf-Blind Perspectives*, alarmingly read:

> An intervener is specially trained to provide clear and consistent sensory information to an individual who is deafblind, compensating for both vision and hearing loss in such a way as to facilitate and enhance learning and interaction with the physical environment and with society. An intervener acts as the eyes and ears of the individual who is deaf-blind, making him or her aware of what is occurring and attaching language and meaning to all experiences. An intervener intercedes between the individual who is deafblind and the environment in such a way so as to minimize the effects of multisensory deprivation, and to empower the individual to have control over his or her life.

This and virtually all other explanations of variously named "sighted guide" or "guide slash interpreter slash teacher" roles make obligatory reference to empowering DeafBlind individuals—it is always "individuals." The conference's keynote speaker, a jovial leader in the Canadian National Society of the Deaf-Blind named Kerry Wadman, stopped joking long enough to remind his audience that "we have dreams and desires, too," and that "Intervention, as we want it, is the provision of an interpretation of what is going on and leaves the final decision up to us."

All I remember of Kerry at the conference was how fast he spoke ASL, how often the audience laughed, and how disappointed I was when, that evening at the banquet, Mom advised against my approaching Kerry, who was by then roaring drunk. I am thankful that a record of the conference proceedings survives, because Kerry's address, titled simply "Intervention," is a fascinating study in missed opportunities. There are openings in the discourse Kerry had offered for our simply seizing the world, but he, like the rest of us, had ceded the world to a sighted person, whose job it was to tell us about it and hand over whatever "final decisions" we made.

Though an ardent advocate of intervention, Kerry was aware of how the ASL word "intervention" is identical to "interruption." He called a part of his speech "Great Interruptions." This section was devoted to hilarious misadventures with Intervenors, and he dexterously used these anecdotes to disrupt his own speech. "So sorry, folks!" he had said, interrupting himself. "There is this thing called intervention." Cue in audience laughter. One story he shared was about the time he was at the subway station. Someone tapped his hand and he reached out, only to have his face slapped. His hand had landed on a lady's bosom. Cue more audience laughter. Kerry continued with his story. Tucking in his hands, he waited for his Intervenor to arrive. When she finally showed up, they left the station and began walking. And they kept walking, until Kerry stopped in his tracks and exclaimed, "Where the hell are we going?"

"Following you, chief!" was the Intervenor's prompt reply.

As I write this, I can feel Kerry throwing up his hands

here for comic effect. Little did he suspect that what he went on to say had stopped short of a very real possibility, something that has now come to pass. But we can honor him for having come so close, and we can understand the shying away that ensued, because we all stopped short for so long. Laughing at his own story, he quipped, "Since when do the blind lead the sighted? I knew of the blind leading the blind, but this was ridiculous!"

II

For about thirty years now, the DeafBlind community in the United States has held two seemingly contradictory positions. One is that access to paid sighted guides—called Support Service Providers, or SSPs for short—is the top issue in our advocacy efforts. Currently, about half the states have an SSP program of some kind. In the states boasting the most developed and well-funded programs, each enrolled DeafBlind person can use fifteen, thirty, or as many as forty-five hours of SSP services per month, which enable us to go shopping, run errands, go through our mail, pursue recreational activities, attend events, and travel. In other cases, we must make do with ten or fewer hours a month. Where there are no SSP programs, we are forced to rely on family, friends, and volunteers, which frequently renders it impossible to do or ask for what we desire. There is no national SSP program. The situation varies from state to state, and many DeafBlind people migrate for the express purpose of living in a state with more SSP services. Wherever there is no such program, we and our friends have lobbied long and hard for this essential resource to be established.

It's an arduous process because hearing-sighted policymakers would rather grant us almost anything else. They have directed millions upon millions of dollars into technology, medical research in the never-ending search for cures, education, pretenses at employment, and even the training of dog guides to the tune of more than fifty thousand dollars per canine. People who sit in cubicles are eager to thrust upon us solutions other than what feels natural and vigorously pragmatic: working with fellow human beings.

The other thing that's just as enduring as our demand for SSP services is our loathing for the term "Support Service Provider." In some countries, more benign or less heavy-handed titles are used, such as "Communicator Guides" in the United Kingdom, "Communication Guides" in Australia, and "Interpreter Guides" in Brazil, though Brazil also has the more problematic "Instructor Mediator" title. But Canada takes the prize for having the most transparent title of all: "Intervenor." The past thirty years has seen a steady stream of proposals in the United States for a new name, including "Access Assistant," "Environmental Information Specialist," "Driver-Guide," and "DeafBlind Services Provider." We all agreed the old name had to go, but we couldn't agree on a replacement. Was a change in terminology all that we wanted, or were we vaguely aware of a deeper problem with the concept of a guide?

When Protactile slid under our arms and tugged, one of the many things that startled us was how inappropriate the theory and practice of guides suddenly seemed to us. Implicit in the act of sighted guiding is the idea that there is one world and one truth, the guide's. Indeed, we had routinely explained to policymakers that SSPs were our eyes. How could we go out there without eyes? The SSP's job was to tell us about the world while steering us away from interfering with it. Grasping our guide's elbow, we glided around like a dream, never making contact with anything or anyone to awaken us.

Sometime around 2010, Terra Edwards, a long-time volunteer SSP and at that time a graduate student, and Jelica Nuccio, her DeafBlind companion for that evening, went to a community event in Seattle. Typically, Terra would have launched into an explanation of what was going on in the room, telling Jelica who was there. On this night, however, Terra asked Jelica to tell her about the environment. Jelica paused, for this was an unusual request. Asking a DeafBlind person for information was something sighted people rarely ever did. As Jelica proceeded to enumerate what she smelled and felt, Terra was, as she later told me, "surprised by how much she had to share with me, and then a feeling of sadness followed." The surface of distantism had been pulled back when Jelica revealed another realm. Terra experienced regret because she had, as a well-schooled sighted associate of our community, worked so eagerly to keep distantism intact. "Now," with the advent of Protactile spaces, she noted, "it is a tactile surface that is broken when distantism breaks through, and the feeling is more one of annoyance."

It was Terra who coined the word for one of the most important new habits for sighted people making the shift away from intervention: not-acting. That is to say, staying chill. If they see a DeafBlind person heading toward a wall, for example, their old impulse is to rush forward and prevent an imagined collision from happening. The reality is that we seek out walls all the time, we bump into things all the time, and we are forever and fluently fumbling. As I repeatedly point out to sighted students of co-navigation, "We go about our business every day, twenty-four hours a day, so why should it suddenly be different because you're there?"

There are two keys to sighted co-navigation, whether one is working as an SSP or moving in another capacity, as a friend, colleague, family member, or partner: not-acting and joining-in instead of intervening. Suppose we enter a room and, while taking off our coat, drop our keys. In the past, a sighted person always pounced to pick up our keys. So consistent was this behavior that if we knew there were sighted people around, we wouldn't bother reaching down to start looking for our keys.

Now, with the Protactile shift, the expectation is that sighted people not-act. They are to continue doing whatever they were doing. We will reach down and start searching for our keys and we will soon find them. In fact, whenever we did go ahead and look for the keys at the same time a sighted person tried to help, either we found them first or the help delayed the retrieval of our keys. We could have been on the verge of grabbing our keys, our fingers a centimeter away, when a sighted person seized our hand, telling us they would get them for us. It never made any difference to them whether we were seemingly going way off or just about to recover our keys. They insisted on taking care of it for us. Why? Because for them, anything we did in our way, the way we did things in private, was the wrong way.

If it happens that we are already with a sighted person, chatting with them, when we drop our keys, our new model of co-navigation dictates that the sighted person do one of the following things: One is to do nothing except maintain co-presence, such as keeping their hand on our back or their leg against our side, as they check their phone or take a sip from their thermos while we fumble for our keys. Or, two, they can signal on our back, to suggest that we fumble toward the left, a little farther up there, bingo! Sometimes this additional information is redundant; sometimes it's helpful. Either way, it is a contribution to, and not a replacement of, our process. Or, three, we can both reach down, our hands together, and when they touch the keys, we also touch them. They are never the one to take up our keys "for us."

At the heart of not-acting and joining-in is the recognition that our way is legitimate. Co-navigation embraces an ecology in which DeafBlind people are a force that shapes the world. The term "co-navigator" points to the fact that there is another navigator, someone else who is also navigating: us. For this reason, much of sighted co-navigation involves doing "nothing." No need to jump up, no need to freak out, no need to swoop down. But it doesn't mean leaving us alone. Quite the opposite: Our process is not exclusive of sighted people. They can join us. They can learn how to fumble along with us. We often want to fumble together.

A mixture of not-acting and joining-in also results in the reversal of who does the most moving around. Sighted people who intervene to help or guide lunge forward, wave at others to get out of the way, call to people from across the room, and fetch things or speak up or take an item off a shelf or open a package or fill a cup or press buttons or carry a tray or throw items into trash cans for, for, for, for, for, for, for, for us. To facilitate the sheer amount of movement they wish to do on our behalf, we were asked to stay and wait. Co-navigation is the opposite. We do most of the moving, routinely leaving sighted co-navigators behind. Because we hated being told to wait, we don't degrade them by parking them. Instead, we talk about when and where we'll rendezvous. "Okay, I'll find you there in about fifteen minutes!"

III

It's no wonder that the grating moniker "Support Service Provider" did not budge until it became much more than a matter of vocabulary. Protactile showed us that something beyond notions of mere access was at stake. People in the movement were busy creating new resonances in our lives when, on June 11, 2018, Jason "Jace" Judy of Ohio sent a message to the Deaf-Blind Studies listserv. It bore the subject line "Do we need to change the SSP term?" Something on Facebook had caught his attention, a proposal to replace the hated term with "Access Provider," and he asked our opinion.

We promptly nixed "Access Provider" and began tossing around alternatives. Some became running jokes, such as the one about our being superheroes with sidekicks. My literary turn of mind found me, on June 21, conjuring up the likes of "Valet," "Chauffeur," "Amanuensis," and "Lieutenant." Somewhat incongruously for this cast of characters, I added "Co-Navigator." I was thinking of the role of ships' navigators in relation to their captains. Upon landing on "Navigator," however, some intuition, a collective filter, nudged me to resist and move beyond the master–servant or executive–assistant symbiosis we had been riffing off of. Indeed, such relationships are apt to flip sides. It must have been the subtlest of impulsions that planted the "Co-" prefix, but once lodged, it was obvious where it had come from. "Co-presence" was already a central concept in our discourse. "Co-creating meaning" had come up a few times, as had "co-conspirator." And we were always talking about navigation.

As I pressed Alt-S and this list of terms slipped into DBS members' inboxes, I decided not to overtly push for

"Co-Navigator." As it happened, I didn't need to. Lisa van der Mark from the Netherlands was the first to second it, or not quite second it, for it hadn't been specifically proposed, but she did lift it out of the tangle of ideas to declare how much she liked it. Tashi Bradford, who was then studying in the United Kingdom, said she still preferred "sidekick." Then a shout came from Ottawa, Ontario, Canada: "Co-Navigator!!!" This was Robert Sirvage, who launched into a discussion of how the term could more deeply inform our movement. Among other things, it was an answer to problematic practices in the field of Orientation and Mobility. Robert recalled for us a conversation he had with a hearing-sighted instructor who specialized in teaching DeafBlind people how to travel with a white cane. He had asked the instructor if he taught Deaf-Blind folks how to walk together with another DeafBlind person. The instructor was dumbfounded.

When Robert asked the instructor how he conducted his lessons, the specialist explained that he would go to a location in advance, such as to a subway station, and map out a route, converting his visual observations of the space into tactile landmarks he then gave his student to follow. After receiving this explanation, Robert inquired of the instructor, "Why not just walk together with your DeafBlind student to check out new places together, and use both of your experiences as a starting point for discussion? So that both of you can build toward an understanding based on what is actually within a DeafBlind person's sensory grasp?"

Once more the specialist was flabbergasted, and the only response he could muster was: "But it would be so unsafe!" After recounting this exchange, Robert again shouted, "Co-Navigator! Love it! This paradigm shift will pave the road for Orientation and Mobility to hire DeafBlind instructors because only we know how to co-navigate. Don't let the guy who uses safety as the reason for everything fool you."

Robert was referring to the Protactile movement's number-one precept when he said "only we know how to co-navigate." If a model requires sight or hearing, it isn't the right model. If it's something that we can do ourselves, then it may be the right way to go. Sighted co-navigation is based on the co-navigating DeafBlind people do together. A sighted person adds an inflection to the process. The way two DeafBlind people co-navigate isn't the same as a sighted person and a DeafBlind person co-navigating, but the point is that the model itself does not require sight or hearing to work.

Almost immediately, we were blessed with the perfect opportunity to test a complete overhaul of "provider" language and thinking. Seven of us Protactile educators gathered in Monmouth, Oregon, during the week of August 6 to 11, 2018, to immerse thirty-six interpreters in our world. We were already going to teach them a very different way of doing "guiding," but now we had a new name. And it was so self-explanatory and suggestive of rich strata of meaning that as we proceeded, we went deeper than we would have without such a designation. One of the educators, Oscar Chacon, wrote to the DeafBlind Studies listserv about his experiences during that whirlwind week. In the beginning, he had felt tense, at odds with the location. But by week's end, he told us, "with the interpreter-trainees becoming our co-navigators, the environments and I were already good friends because I had partners to complement their receptions of environmental stimuli with my own, which I shared as well." He felt like he and the universe had finally clicked. "The astonishing multiplying power of Protactile!"

"Great post!" jumped in H. L. Pavey from Texas. "I had to do a fist-bump in the air and internally say 'YES!' when I saw the word 'co-navigators.' That's a term I want to experience a lot more!" She then noted how society does love acronyms and jokingly wondered if it is to be "CONG." "I'm a little bit silly here, excuse me!" The settled acronym proved to be the much duller "CN," but it quickly gained wide circulation. During the ensuing year, a comprehensive theoretical exploration of co-navigation anchored the discourse within the Protactile movement.

On July 28, 2019, Victoria Magliocchino, president of the Florida DeafBlind Association, asked the DeafBlind Studies community for input. The board of directors had brought up the need to get rid of the "SSP" term for a program they ran. Vicky had suggested replacing it with "CN," and reported that, "The board seems to like the term 'co-navigator,' but they want to make sure the term is appropriate. I explained my reason: A DeafBlind person co-navigates with a sighted person and they work together to gain access."

On August 12, 2019, the earth shook with the news that our new term had been formally adopted by an organization for the first time. In her celebratory message, Vicky wrote:

I am very excited to announce we the Florida DeafBlind Association (FDBA) Board have agreed to change the term Support Service Provider (SSP) to CoNavigator (CN). The new term shows that the CN works WITH the DeafBlind individual, making her or him autonomous.

FSSP is now FCN—Florida CoNavigators. No hyphen, just like "DeafBlind."

IV

The emergence of Protactile is such an epoch-maker that there
is a Before and an After. We who are in the After regard Before
with disbelief, laughter, and outrage. What went on Before is
the stuff of slapstick comedy or historical trauma or, not infre-
quently, both. When we bring up something from Before,
those of us who were there will say, "Whatever were they
thinking? Why didn't we know?" Those who only know the
After are incredulous: "How is it possible anyone thought that
was a good idea?" As it happens, what SSPs did—and continue to do, if they haven't changed or been fired—provokes
the most gasps of both mock and genuine horror: "No way!
Really? Impossible!"

Before, each time an SSP came to pick us up, they stepped
out of their car, walked up to our door or the entrance to our
building, tapped our shoulder, and, after a greeting, gave us
their elbow. We took it and followed them to the passenger
side of their car, whereupon they opened the door for us, often
holding our head down like a police officer does on television.
In the worst cases, we were expected not to close the door but
to let the SSP close it. This was low-grade torture, because our
natural inclination was to reach out to make sure the door
was closed but at the moment we reached out to find out what
was going on with the door or why it was taking longer for
the SSP to close it than we anticipated it would take, the door
sometimes slammed on our inquiring hand. There were also
horror stories—considered as such even back then—where an
SSP put on our seat belt for us.

After, when a CN picks us up, we typically have them wait
inside their car as we go out to meet their car. We feel our way

to the passenger-side door, open it, and reach in to make sure it's them. The CN says "Hey you!" or gives a thumbs up, and we slide into our seat. We may greet them first before closing the passenger-side door, or we may close the door first before turning to greet them. We put on our seat belt ourselves.

Before, while holding on to an SSP's elbow as we walked along sidewalks, they occasionally stooped to indicate that we should stoop behind them, or else they tried to pull us down. This was for us to avoid hitting our head against a low tree limb hanging over our path. The awkward procedure rarely worked. For example, the SSP often stood up once they were safely beyond the tree limb's leafy reach, only to have us stand up at the same time, knocking our head on it anyway.

After, with a CN walking side by side with us, our hands together, always communicating, they mention that there's a tree. We both reach up to touch the tree's shivering lushness. It is the simplest thing in the world to pass under the tree limb while or just after touching it.

Before, during more than a million combined trips to grocery stores over forty years of the Support Service Provider era, the SSP routinely took the front end of a shopping cart to pull it while we held on to the handle behind the cart. Thus we followed the cart on its hypnotizing wending way through the store. It stopped now and then for the SSP, consulting our shopping list, to put items in our cart or to ask us a question. "For Rice Chex, do you want family size or regular size?" A troubling trend was how the SSP treated our shopping list as a source of authority greater than we ourselves were. When we changed our mind, such as dropping red plums in favor of fresher black plums, they told us, "No, your list says red plums!"

After, with CNs, we both walk behind the shopping cart

together, always communicating. When we stop, we both reach for an item, and it is we who take it down from its shelf and place it in the cart. We roam around with our hands regularly as our CN adds information about what we are touching. Many times we feel for something without the CN knowing, or needing to know, what we are looking for. We ourselves may not always know and may be curious, or we do know, we know what the item feels like among its counterparts.

Before, an SSP always freaked out when there was a slip or an accident, such as our colliding with a pole after they had looked away. "Oh, I'm so sorry! I wasn't paying attention! It's my fault!" Operating as "providers" as they did, they wielded a great deal of control, but it also came with an awful, self-absorbed sense of responsibility. Actually, they apologized so ardently it's a wonder "SSP" didn't stand for "Sorry Sighted Person."

After, when we're walking with a CN and a pole hits our shoulder, they pause. If we shrug it off and continue, we continue. They don't say anything about it. They don't freak out. This is because our bumping into things is the norm, and they recognize that. We are still responsible, we still do our own navigating. Just because we are with a CN doesn't mean we stop navigating, stop using our cane, stop attending to the fact that we are two people journeying together, covering for ourselves and each other. If we get hurt, the CN asks, "Are you all right? Where does it hurt? Oh no! Do you want ice for that?" This is the concern and care of a fellow traveler.

Before, an SSP asked us what we wanted from the bank teller, and, upon learning the transactions we wished to be made, they proceeded to engage with the bank teller. The SSP told the teller to make this deposit or that withdrawal. From time to time, the SSP asked us for our identification card or relayed to us a question the teller had that the SSP didn't know the answer to. If a silence stretched on for too long and we asked what was going on, they often said, "Wait, I'm talking to the teller" or "Explain later." Also, it was always to the SSP that the teller said "Good morning" or "Have a nice day." The SSP always responded in kind, sometimes letting us know what the teller had said too late for us to say "You have a nice day, too."

After, our CN does not ask us in advance what we want to accomplish at the bank. When we approach a teller, the CN gives us a quick sketch of who the teller is—their appearance, race, gender, approximate age, general disposition, the name on their tag—and what they're doing. "Now she's looking up at us, smiling. Says, How can I help you today?" We may, for example, reach over to take the teller's hand and gesture with it to request paper and a pen. Our CN says, "She understands. Now looking for a piece of paper. Found one, handing it over—toward me." The CN does not take the piece of paper, but merely reports the fact that the teller had handed it over to them. We take the piece of paper, to establish and continue a direct link with the teller. Our taking initiative for every stage of every interaction leads to the building of relationships, such as with a bank teller whose name we remember the next time, and "Good morning" evolves into "How are your kids doing" and "Shh, here, I got this chocolate bar for you. When I saw it, I thought of you!"

Before, it was always smooth sailing with an SSP, every task and every interaction successful. But successful for whom?

After, with a CN, as well as without one, we experience failures sometimes. Co-navigation brings us into contact with wonderful people as well as people who are rude, inflexible, and unwilling to engage. Such ruptures mean we are in thrilling commerce with reality. And it means we take matters into our own hands, deciding whether we want to walk out, demand to talk with the manager, fight it out with the rude person.

Before, in fast-food or buffet-style establishments or the like, often an SSP stood up and said, "I'm going to refill my cup. Want me to refill your cup, too? Can I get you anything else?"

After, in the same sorts of places, we often stand up and say to our seated CN, "I'm going to refill my cup. Want me to refill your cup, too? Can I get you anything else?" Or, as a matter of common courtesy, a CN may do the same for us. When we stress in our teaching that sighted co-navigators shouldn't do things "for" us, one frequent response from novices is, "But I'm a very polite person. I do those things for anyone, not just for a DeafBlind person! It's not helping, it's being nice!"

To which we reply, "Yes, but is your relationship with the DeafBlind people reciprocal in that we can also extend such kindnesses to you in return?" For the sighted-guide model is nothing if not designed to ensure that we never gain enough purchase on the environment to harvest it for ourselves and be generous to others. Co-navigation involves both of us touching the environment, including the soda fountain, or else our proceeding to explore on our own.

V

In 1928, a British-Irish DeafBlind writer and her friends founded the National Deaf-Blind Helpers' League, the world's first formal human-guide service for DeafBlind people. It was a successful undertaking—the organization eventually became Deafblind UK, the country's largest and most

comprehensive provider of services, training, and housing—
but it wasn't without causes for concern. The writer, Frieda
Le Pla, later published an autobiographical and sociological
study called *Glimpses Into a Hidden World*. One of the things
that worried her was "de-personalization." Frieda let a cor-
respondent of hers, "Mavis," sum it up for her readers. Mavis
had written:

> Since deafness added itself to blindness I have often had
> occasion to feel as if I had ceased to be a real human being,
> a *person*, and had become instead just a physical body that
> needs only to be fed now and then, and kept housed and
> warm, and could then be ignored as a ghost or shadow,
> with no right to be consulted about anything, and no intel-
> lect or soul to be taken into account.

And Kerry Wadman, in the middle of his adulatory account
of intervention during the 1996 conference that I attended,
inserted a remark reinforcing Mavis's incisive thought. He said
that DeafBlind people often felt sorry for hearing and sighted
people, especially Intervenors. "People who can see and hear,"
he explained, "tend to concentrate on communicating to,
directing, guiding, helping, and teaching us . . . to the point
where our humanity gets lost." My friend Erin Manning, an
artist and philosopher, once observed with me that what happens when someone thinks someone else needs "help" is that
"the world is reduced, it becomes *less*." Everyone is supposed
to be affected by every interaction we have, to change another
and be changed by them as well as to change the environment
around us and be changed by it. But intervention, as a process in "subtraction" of the world, requires that sighted guides
become hardened and finds us becoming hard, too. Nowhere

is this truth more chillingly—if unconsciously—stated than the section heading in the latest published definition of SSP services, from June 2021, that reads: "SSP Philosophy: Professional Distance, Objectivity, Respect."

In the United States the harm went further when our traditional helpers were split into two classes: interpreters and SSPs. In many parts of the world, while "interpreting" and "guiding" are recognized as different tasks, both are performed by the same person. What caused this intuitive organization of human resources to be torn asunder?

When the American Association of the DeafBlind began hosting annual national conventions in 1975, the organization recruited many volunteers to support an awkward approach by which they followed sighted conferencing norms as much as possible. To make this work, most of the volunteers were called upon to do interpreting during presentations and meetings. Meanwhile, interpreters for sighted Deaf people were agitating to get their work recognized as a profession, complete with formal training and certification. Certified interpreters enlisted to support AADB conventions felt they should be distinguished from volunteers who were not trained or certified interpreters. In 1980, the AADB president Roderick Macdonald came up with "Support Service Provider" as a label for any convention helper who wasn't an "Interpreter." Thus was the Great Split born.

At first, the "Support Service Provider" tag was attached to anyone who supported the conventions: those who loaded luggage onto buses, those who served food in the cafeteria, those who worked the registration tables, those who set up or cleared off chairs, as well as those who worked more closely with the DeafBlind delegates. Over time and beyond the conventions, as more and more interpreters said it wasn't their job to drive us or guide us or describe the environment, "Support Service Provider" came to mean a lower-level professional or volunteer who did many things but not interpreting. There's a moment in Joanne Greenberg's highly ethnographic 1988 novel *Of Such Small Differences* that captures a classic example of the Great Split at work. Joanne is a trained anthropologist, and to create her main DeafBlind character, John, along with other people in his world, she interviewed many delegates, volunteers, and interpreters at the 1986 AADB convention. John has the following exchange with an interpreter when they step outside after an appointment. Finding that it's raining hard, with some walking, a bus ride, and more walking to reach home ahead of him, John turns to the interpreter and asks:

"Can you give me a ride home?"

There was a pause and then her wet hands answered, "I'm not local here; I'm from California."

"Are you leaving for there now?"

"No, I meant something else. I meant I'm a professional. We're trying to establish interpreting as a profession. You wouldn't expect your doctor or lawyer to provide transportation."

"I'm not asking you to provide transportation, I'm asking for a ride. Is it out of your way?"

"Even if it wasn't, that's not the point. The point is professionalism. Professionalism and insurance." She left him.

Interpreters ceasing to drive us to and from appointments, meetings, classes, and events, as well as the people we do carpool with ceasing to be interpreters, has cost us untold opportunities, educations, careers, and lives. Throughout my many failed attempts to gain a university education, for example, interpreters were always waiting there in the classroom, ready to work. But I could never attend class regularly, because bus drivers routinely failed to stop for me or forgot to tell me when we arrived at my desired bus stop, or because paratransit arrived late to pick me up or had many other stops before dropping me off. Even when I started receiving SSP services, which involved an SSP picking me up for us to run errands around town, it did not offer a solution for my schooling. "The policy," the SSP program director told me, "is that you cannot use an SSP just for a ride. If you go to a class, there is nothing for the SSP to do there, and that is not the purpose of the service. If you go to a grocery store, that's fine, because the SSP will be guiding you in the store. Is that clear?"

More serious is our common and deep reluctance to seek medical care because it's so hard and rarely works out to arrange for an appointment, arrange for an interpreter to be there, and arrange for a ride, this last crucial link frequently the definition of "fail"—such as the medical van driver yelling at us and then leaving because we didn't respond. My dearest childhood role model besides my father, Leslie Peterson, died at age sixty-six. He had put off seeing a doctor until it was too late. By then, the cancer was too advanced. Some years before, he had told me that he thought he had lived through a heart attack. When the chest squeeze came and he started to sweat profusely, he went to his recliner and commended himself to God. He joked that he had been disappointed he hadn't died then.

The professionalization of interpreters was a powerful

process that benefited sighted Deaf people, resulting in interpreting services and access to distance telecommunications being guaranteed by such legislation as 1990's landmark Americans with Disabilities Act. "Guiding services" were never included, nor was tactile access to telecommunications. We were left out, and could only use what is designed for and guaranteed to sighted Deaf people. While the co-navigational framework is for everyone, so far the title of "CoNavigator" has been mainly used to replace "Support Service Provider." This leaves the Great Split intact. But should it? Shouldn't we extend the framework to include those formerly contained in the role of interpreters, thus sewing back together what, as we turn it over, had been cut in two?

It was my left eyelid that gave me my first taste of a world where I had a CoNavigator rather than an SSP and, separately, an interpreter. A bump in my lower eyelid was bothering me. It turned out to be a sty, a mundane affliction I'd never experienced before. It wasn't painful enough for the emergency room but was becoming annoying enough to contemplate the hassle of making an appointment with my doctor. The appointment was set for two days later, but the irritation soon became unbearable. I emailed Ico, who's one of my regular CNs, paid for by a consumer-directed program. I'd converted Ico into a CN. They were available that evening, and I emailed the interpreting services coordinator at my clinic to say I wanted to do a walk-in during Urgent Care hours. And, I told the coordinator, I knew an interpreter who was available. Ico happens to be a certified interpreter as well, which most SSPs are not. The clinic would pay for Ico the interpreter and the consumer-directed fund under my control would pay Ico for the time before and after the visit at the clinic, but in my mind, I had an experiment. What if clinics, universities, agencies, and other places offered CNs so we could navigate their systems as a whole?

I opened the passenger-side door. "You got it!" Ico said. I jumped in, and we zipped through light traffic.

The receptionist at the clinic on Wabasha Street was sheepish. "So sorry, it'll take maybe two hours, maybe longer." Ico told me there were eight people in the waiting room.

"Do you know," I wondered, bidding Ico to interpret, "if the wait is shorter at another clinic?"

The reception smiled. "I'll make some calls and see what I can do." A minute later, she said, "The Como Park location has a fifteen-minute wait."

"Thanks a million!" I directed at her and, privately to Ico, said, "Let's go."

Como Park was a fifteen-minute drive, the wait was ten minutes, and I only had a sty. "Nothing to be done," the doctor chuckled. "Just an opiate eye drop. Over the counter. It'll heal in six weeks." He laughed again when I gripped his leg in response to "six weeks."

The pain had disappeared by then—whether due to the relief of knowing what it was or due to the ease of the whole experience I don't know. We stopped at a random pharmacy and I grabbed the box of eye drops. Because I was out instead of cooking supper for my family, I decided to do a drive-through at Culver's and bring home burgers and fries for everyone.

On the way home, with the smell of supper wafting into my nostrils and my left lower eyelid blinking more comfortably, I said to Ico, "You know, those people in the waiting room back there at the Wabasha clinic . . . They all probably have a car, right? So why are they waiting there for hours when they can go to Como Park or wherever?"

"Yeah!" Ico laughed. "But, to be honest with you, it'd have never occurred to me to do that. Thanks to you I know what to do next time that happens to me."

OF MASKS AND
BLINDFOLDS

When the first COVID-19 mask mandates went into effect, there arose a great and terrible cry. This wasn't the howl of conservatives chafing against perceived governmental overreach. It came from Deaf people finding it unexpectedly harder to understand each other and hearing people in person. American Sign Language derives most of its grammar not from a speaker's winged hands but from their facial expressions— eye gaze, eyelid flutterings and squintings, eyebrow configurations, cheek puffs, the wrinkling or curling or flaring of nostrils, and what is called "mouthing," itself a whole galaxy of gestures. While ASL speakers knew, theoretically, how important those "non-manual markers" were, masks proved it in a most palpable way.

As Deaf social media flooded with their frustrations, we DeafBlind folks couldn't help guffawing. Now they are having a taste, we told one another, of what we had to put up with all those years. We had long been expected to move our hands through empty air, hoping that our sighted interlocutors were indeed listening, and to take ASL in by placing our hands over theirs. And they became upset with us whenever we misunderstood them, which was often. "No, I told you to put it there!" "No, I said seven-thirty!" Our faces burned with shame, and we couldn't figure out how we'd failed to comprehend. Weren't we fluent in the language? Hadn't we distinctly felt what their hands had said?

The truth is that one cannot sustain fluency in a sign language without sight, and just getting the hands is to grasp about one third of the language. No wonder, then, that there emerged in our midst a new language based on contact not just with hands but also with arms, shoulders, chests, and, when sitting, legs, a language anchored not just by tactile reception but also by proprioception. We could not go on with crumbs of auditory and visual languages. Protactile is our first native language, native in the sense that it flows from our intuitions and our reality. Thanks to Protactile, we realized what a slippery enterprise it had been to read ASL through the hands alone.

Aware that many ASL speakers were scrambling to make masks with plastic windows so they could see more of each other's grammatical faces, I was curious what it'd be like to meet a sighted friend for the first time in the mask era. Well, the first friend I talked with in Protactile felt—that is to say, they looked, sounded, smiled, groaned, snickered, shrugged, fumed, and laughed—exactly the same. Their mask made no difference to me. It was as if they weren't wearing one at all. They appeared in their full glory.

My own mask, however, surprised me. I found it relaxing because I no longer had to be as mindful of my face in the presence of a sighted person. True, Protactile had helped us let go of the faces we used to have that went with speaking ASL, English, or any other language, in any culture. My ASL "mask" had begun to grow heavy as soon as the warm and voluble visages around me withdrew from view. I remember thinking to myself, "My face is falling off." The difficulty in remembering to frown when posing a question or to puff my cheeks to punctuate a statement caused me to fall silent in ASL spaces. My presentations ran shorter and shorter than planned. Then, at a conference, my hands dropped after ten minutes and I hurriedly wrapped up what was supposed to be an hour-long talk. My Deaf partner was also a presenter at the conference, and after watching my aborted talk, she gently said, "You should never present in ASL again." Her nudge was what I needed to take the radical and, once taken, all too logical step of declining to address a large audience directly. On October 20, 2017, the date of that year's Deaf Social Justice Conference, I became the first person to present in Protactile in such a setting, by inviting a DeafBlind friend to sit with me on the stage to receive my talk and by letting interpreters translate my content into ASL and English for the benefit of the audience. It felt so good to gallop for a full hour again, this time as the headless horseman!

So I had already long abandoned my ASL mask when I put on a pandemic mask for the first time. What the cloth covering relieved me of was another mask, a more general assembling of an "appropriate" face. Per sighted norms, I knew I shouldn't twist my lips in front of sighted people, or bare my teeth because I wanted to stretch my cheek muscles, or stick out my tongue because it felt good to do it at the moment. Behind the mask, those parts of my face were thrilled to pursue their diverse lives. I suddenly appreciated what my fellow

Protactile educator Jaz Herbers had meant when he explained why he favored dark sunglasses. He had initially put them on to blot out the little light perception he still had, which had been annoying him, but he discovered another advantage. He no longer had to think about his eyes. "I don't want anyone to gaze into my eyes and go 'Oh I see,'" he said. Being more visually inscrutable, he had learned from his shades and I was now learning from my mask, was yet another way to subvert sighted norms.

Did some sighted people continue trying to read things off Jaz's face despite his dark shades? It tickled me to think of the rest of Jaz's face disappearing behind a mask. It only reinforces the same demand that others listen to us. For where else are we present if not where we reciprocate? Sensing this, sighted students of Protactile routinely and voluntarily blindfold themselves in order to pay attention. To fully appreciate the sweetness with which those swaths of fabric float up to envelop their eyes, it's worth considering the sour taste the fetching of blindfolds has traditionally left in our mouths. Untold millions of sighted people go through simulation activities—in elementary school classrooms, interpreter training programs, medical schools, corporate and nonprofit sensitivity trainings, and college and certificate programs that churn out sighted teachers of the blind, occupational therapists, Orientation and Mobility instructors, and vocational rehabilitation counselors—and come out giddy with the novelty of being blind for ten minutes, or feeling confused and embarrassed, or convinced that blindness is an unbearable tragedy. Studies have shown that disability simulations are deeply misguided and misguiding, consistently producing unintended negative outcomes.

One of my sighted Protactile-speaking friends, Wendy Harris, has experienced and witnessed multiple simulations involving blindfolds while pursuing certification as a teacher of the blind. "Sudden, significant change of any kind," she reflected during a discussion we had on the topic, "is usually hard to deal with." She continued: "However, ten minutes of experiencing this big change to their usual way of doing things is not long enough to adjust to a new normal and build new skills. The person is just left with the experience of shock and difficulty. Leading to pity."

And, in some cases, leading to trauma. Julie Hochgesang, a professor of linguistics at Gallaudet University, often tells the story of her worst experience as the only Deaf student in a public school. In fourth grade, her class read about Helen Keller, and the teacher had everyone take turns being blindfolded and having their ears muffled. At first Julie was frightened, but as she watched her fellow students laughing and supporting each other, she raised a trembling hand to be the next volunteer. As Julie remembers it, she shook violently when she wrapped the blindfold around her eyes and started to walk around. In her words:

> I could feel the corners of the desks, the rounded metal backs of chairs, the hardness of the school floor as I scuffled about with my arms raised in front of me . . . I didn't feel the softness or warmth of a single human body. It felt like it had been ages—but it was probably three minutes—that I walked around slowly, trying to find people. Finally I lifted up my blindfold. Not a person was in the classroom. They were all gathered at the door staring at me and laughing. Apparently the school bell had rung and they thought it'd be funny to leave me wandering about . . . I felt my face become as red as fire and to this day, I still can't be blindfolded or trust a room of people enough to look out for me.

Some sighted people have shared with me that they found all their simulation experiences to be powerful. One interpreter reported remembering every single simulation exercise she went through, even years afterward, and termed the effect they created "visceral memory." She felt the simulations were what drove necessary lessons home. "But," I openly wondered during our conversation, "is what got burned into your psyche what we want you to carry around?" Another interpreter contended during one of my seminars that her encounter with a blindfold in a class some years before had benefitted her greatly. "We had to make a peanut butter and jelly sandwich while blindfolded," she said. "It took me FOREVER, but I learned a million things in the process!" The problem, I pointed out in response, is that what it's like for us to make the same sandwich isn't one of the million things she had learned. It's a false equivalency.

To anyone protesting that those simulations can be done "right," by emphasizing to participants that they are not learning what it's like to be blind but are learning other things, the question must be asked: What about those of us who are already blind? Will we learn those intended lessons by participating in the activity? If we won't receive the same pedagogical benefits, what does that tell us about the nature of the simulations? Whatever the lessons that need to be learned, surely there are more meaningful and realistic ways to achieve those results. Perhaps the most notable alternative to false sensory simulation is Deaf Strong Hospital, a day-long workshop conducted every fall since 1998 for first-year medical school students at the University of Rochester. Instead of having the future doctors wear earplugs to experience sudden and temporary deafness, they remain hearing and enter an environment. Deaf Strong Hospital mimics a typical medical setting, only all the people role-playing doctors, nurses, and receptionists are Deaf people speaking ASL. The bewildered medical students, playing "patients," are faced with consent forms printed in a random foreign written language, doctors who add one misdiagnosis on top of another because the patients can't communicate back in ASL, and barriers that persist even after they're finally assigned an interpreter. This is a major shift away from sensory simulations that suggest a disability is the problem rather than structures and processes in place.

My long-standing skepticism toward sensory simulation exercises means I don't thrust blindfolds upon my students. Yet many instinctively reach for them in their wish to attend to touch, to be more immersed, to gain focus. After all, aren't eyeballs forever being tugged here and there in our intensely ocularcentric society? As Theresa B. Smith, a sighted interpreter educator and the author of the seminal textbook *Guidelines: Practical Tips for Working and Socializing with Deaf-Blind People*, explained, it can be a "brain bandwidth" issue. Theresa herself, for example, found that shutting out vision makes her suddenly aware of smells. "Ordinarily," she shared with me, "I'm pretty oblivious to smells and have even had a DeafBlind friend tease me when I didn't notice the odor of some old food. I said my nose was 'hard-of-smelling' and he replied that no, my nose was 'deaf.'" Heather Holmes, my sighted colleague at the Protactile Language Interpreting National Education Center, expanded on Theresa's point by referring to Cognitive Load Theory. It postulates that we all have a "working memory" that figures out how and where to store new information. How well that process works depends on the difficulty of the content encountered, how that content is presented, and whether we have previous schemas that allow us to quickly store information until we can develop a stronger command of the content.

If the content is dense, or it is poorly and confusingly presented, or we lack schemas to temporarily and helpfully put it aside to allow us to continue absorbing even more information, our working memory can get jammed. "As a sighted person," Heather said while considering the process of learning not just a new language but one in a new modality, "if I am trying to take in visual information, tactile information, and environmental information, all while trying to learn something new that I have no schema for, this overloads the working memory." She continued:

> Putting on a blindfold essentially forces a lower extrinsic cognitive load, that is to say, it forces a sighted person to only focus on the sensory stimulus of touch. The person is not trying to use *all* of their senses and so their sensory memory is not overloaded. The blindfold helps to decrease the extrinsic cognitive load while a person is developing a new schema.

When a sighted person becomes more comfortable with tactile reception, it is less likely they will need a blindfold as an aid. They may achieve what we have termed "soft focus," where they do continue to use their vision but are able to receive information through touch at the same time. Heather cautioned that this doesn't mean the sighted student who is able to background vision and foreground touch is now an expert in tactile reception. "If you gave me a blindfold, I know I would struggle and it would take significant time and practice to become proficient," she cheerily confessed. "But I have no trouble focusing on touch without a blindfold, and I am not overwhelmed by tactile information, because I already have a developed schema and I can then store new information I am learning in that schema!"

One specific function of immersion blindfolding is to mute others' noisy faces—the murmuring faces of hearing English speakers, the virtuoso symphonies of ASL faces, and the mumbling of DeafBlind people's faces at varying stages of abandoning visual communication. Since pandemic masks inadvertently perform this favor, sighted students can find themselves partially blindfolded anyway, unable to rely on others' faces for information. Nightfall offers the same service every day. Power outages occasionally throw in their share. A flick of a light switch can provide the treat. For our part, many DeafBlind students of Protactile also need all of those blindfoldings. Those of us who grew up with some eyesight were conditioned to squeeze as much out of it as possible, to the last prismatic drop. Sighted people generally have an easier time heeding Jaz's famous admonition to "Leave your eyeballs at the door!" In full possession of sight privilege, they can gently dim their vision. As it happens, the Protactile word "sighted" is synonymous with "unblindfolded."

It isn't the aim of Protactile to unmask sighted people as being blinded by sight, as it were, but it is a natural by-product of the movement to help everyone realize that we're all blindfolded. Unlike many who have the progressive-blindness condition Usher syndrome, I went tactile long before it was the last remaining course. For example, I could have continued to watch the ground ahead of me for many more years before finally picking up a white cane. There were many reasons why I'd gone tactile early, chief among them the many Deaf-Blind role models I was blessed to know through my father's involvement in our community. Very few DeafBlind children grow up with such role models. One lure for my going tactile, though, was the sheer beauty of my alma mater.

Founded in 1863, the Minnesota State Academy for the Deaf rests atop a tree-filled bluff, with all its limestone buildings facing each other across a spacious green. The one-way street that runs around the green is punctuated on both sides by green lampposts with white globes that shine orange-yellow at night. The whole scene called me to lift up my poor eyes. I wrapped this brilliant and living postcard picture around my eyes as I went tactile. After thirty years I still remember walking out of Smith Hall after school one autumn afternoon. I looked up at the limestone façade of Tate Hall, resplendent in slanting light with its white trim, green shutters, impossibly long slate roof, and blazing cupola. My mask was already loosening, and as I scraped my cane's tip back and forth across the sidewalk, I felt fallen leaves clustering around my shoes. They tumbled aside readily enough, but one or two leaves clung on a little longer before letting go.

PART THREE

A DIFFERENT
CENTER
OF GRAVITY

THE TEXTURE OF
VIRTUAL TOUCH

"The cure cannot be worse than the problem." Those who wanted to end social distancing seized on this tagline and other arguments. For a fleeting moment, I felt perfect sympathy with those sentiments. Compulsory social distancing is indeed a nightmare for DeafBlind people. For us, making a transaction through a pane of glass or greeting someone six feet away isn't an option.

That's why several media outlets—ABC News, the *Washington Post*, and the *New Yorker* notable among them—rushed to gawk at DeafBlind people and our supposed plight during the COVID-19 pandemic. None of the stories got it right about the impact on our community. They had no message nor did they discuss any solutions. Instead, those pieces served only as sadness parades, a spectacle, perhaps helping the more privileged feel relieved that they're in a better position.

It is true that the virus has thrown many of us off balance.

Sighted people are keeping themselves out of reach. People stand in lines impossible for us to follow. Hospitals roll in video screens showing interpreters we can neither see nor touch. Pedestrians pass us by, refusing to walk across an intersection with us. Those of us who live alone can go for weeks, even months, without touching anyone.

None of which, however, is anything new. Those things were true before the COVID-19 outbreak. In many ways, the stay-at-home and social distancing mandates merely formalize what our community has been experiencing all along. Long before COVID-19, I wrote the essay called "Distantism," which appears earlier in this book, that defined and named— you guessed it—social distancing. I discussed the irony of how the Internet is supposed to connect everyone but often ends up isolating people from one another. This means distantism goes deeper than whether or not we are in physical contact. It has everything to do with *how* our beings spill one into another, be it in person or virtually, with words or gestures or any kind of action, through any medium. We've long lived in a society committed to independence, individualism, and ownership of property. The Latin word "distantia" means "a standing apart." Capitalism loves distantism because it replaces community with consumption. Distantism privileges the distance senses of sight and hearing to the exclusion of other ways of being in the world. There has been a steady trend in making touch taboo, where the answer to inappropriate contact is to simply ban all touch, including the kinds that are indispensable to childhood development and adult mental health.

It's no accident that social distancing is the major response to the spread of the virus, after our federal government failed to execute any number of earlier possible responses to contain it. We already live in a society designed for people who stay apart. Touch is considered disposable. Our governments have never been good with multiple, nuanced solutions. They always go for the One Answer. We also live in a society that's very comfortable with leaving people behind.

Before the pandemic, we in the Protactile movement were flying around to all parts of our country and abroad teaching about our language and practices. Now, suddenly, all those trips to teach the world how to touch were canceled. That shook me, and I wondered what would become of the world we were building. For a while I could not bear to read on Twitter what sighted people were saying. #AloneTogether. Zoom Zoom Zoom. No Contact Is Sexy!

As life went on and we continued talking, I felt much better. So did others. Take Bruce Visser, a DeafBlind master carpenter and committed outdoorsman from Seattle. When the topic of COVID-19 came up, his immediate comment was:

> I believe the DeafBlind community in many ways is ahead of the curve. Our unique upbringings taught us many things, thought processes and skills that are fluid enough to be applied in many areas. Nothing is ever smooth navigating but each and every lesson has a value, it is up to us individually, collectively and in villages across the globe how to embrace and appreciate the valuable nuggets we either learned or to be learned.

And Jelica Nuccio, my friend and the founder of Tactile Communications in Monmouth, Oregon, noted that "Coronavirus is really having a big impact on everyone. The one bright spot is that DeafBlind people already know how to live like this. Other people, however, are not used to it. Everyone needs to support each other."

What are Bruce and Jelica talking about? Touch, of course. Not just physical contact or tactile communication, but the act of reaching out. And we know how to do that virtually as well as in person.

A key moment in the formation of our community occurred around 1850, when Laura Bridgman, then the most famous DeafBlind person, and Morrison Heady began corresponding with each other. Morrison was a DeafBlind poet, novelist, inventor, architect, businessman, and advocate from Louisville, Kentucky, who had already constructed his identity as a DeafBlind person. His 1853 long poem "The Double Night" is one of the most important texts in our literature. He started reaching out to other DeafBlind people, partly to share one of his inventions, the alphabet glove. It had buttons sewn on it representing letters that people could "type" on to communicate with us.

The communications and transportation revolutions of 1815–1848—which brought modern printing, the telegraph, the steamboat, and railroads—made possible raised type and Braille embossing, various mechanical writing methods, and an increasingly affordable and speedy postal service. Ours was still a rural country, and it was too hard to gather in person. But that didn't stop us from establishing our community—virtually—via correspondence networking. By the time Morrison met Laura in person for the first time in 1854, they had already developed a close relationship as "letter-friends." Laura and Morrison kept in touch until her death in 1889, but Morrison was able to visit her in person only one other time, in 1859.

The young Helen Keller knew him as "Uncle Morrie," who wrote her stories. Correspondence networks begat Braille publications, and those gave birth to our first incorporated organizations. Our discourse has never required that we meet in person. Of course, we found ways to gather more and more often in person, thanks to urbanization, airplanes, public transportation, and interpreting and sighted assistant services. But even today, we do most of our communing virtually, through hundreds of local, national, and international email groups. Web-based social media, often inaccessible and highly visual in design, has never surpassed the ease and utility of email. Email works wonderfully with our need for key commands, which are the way we navigate via Braille on a computer or with devices in lieu of mouses, track pads, or "touch screens." It is marvelous how much joy we can create through text only, "exchanging words to tell the tale of the little rhythms each of us produces in the vast chorus that is existence," as my friend Christopher Phillips from West Virginia recently put it.

I am part of more than a dozen email groups and I moderate five. My most formative experience with an email community was with a bunch of DeafBlind poets. We called ourselves GIPers after the name of our listserv, DB-GoldInPoetry. I cut my political teeth on the American Association of the Deaf-Blind listserv. DeafBlind Studies is an intellectual hotbed. If you're single, there's an email hookup hub. Once, on one listserv, there was a wild, epic adventure cruise that lasted *five years*, taking members from imaginary island to imaginary island and through many a shipwreck. Admiral Kiss, Hippie, Moses, Momma Nature, De Jester, the Librarian, and other nicknamed participants will live on forever in community lore. Although the Twin Cities, where I live, has one of the most active local communities in terms of meetings and gatherings in person, our local listserv, DBMinn, is a vital space. We have volunteers responsible for posting different kinds of information. One posts a daily weather report. Another posts sports scores. Another posts the day's news briefs from the Minneapolis *Star Tribune*. Representatives from various agencies, programs, and organizations share updates, newsletters, and legislative alerts and calls for action. Text flyers for upcoming events let us know about in-person events. Always there is a great deal of joyful chatter, punctuated by the occasional controversy and drama. When COVID-19 broke out, DBMinn became even more crucial: daily numbers, explanations of risks, updates from the governor's office, lists of what was open, offers of help, sharing with each other what we were doing, and discussing how to adapt.

For a while, millions of sighted people also connected through listservs, before Facebook and other social media platforms took over their screen time. But it has always been different for us. Generally speaking, we don't have telephones, TV, movies, radio, or easy access to newspapers. So our listservs had to fulfill those needs, along with our chatter and work on community projects. We developed our own etiquette around emails, and even our own lingo. The most popular example of the latter is "LOY," a spin on LOL that means "laughing on you," reflective of how we backchannel laughter in person by wiggling our fingers on a speaker's body.

Until recently, very few people outside of our community ever knew what we were up to in our virtual spaces. When my work in DeafBlind and Protactile studies attracted invitations to teach courses, I realized that I wanted to do it only in two ways. One is in Protactile space, through Protactile, and in Protactile format, in person, where everyone maintains co-presence. No distantism allowed. The other way is to teach "online"—but not by using any websites or fancy multipurpose platforms. I use an email listserv, thus immersing my sighted students in our traditional DeafBlind virtual space.

When people register for a class, I add their email addresses to a secure and private listserv devoted to the course. While I do follow a syllabus, which has a schedule, there are no fixed times that folks must show up. They can read the posts when they can, at their own pace. They can respond when they like. Order isn't important—they can respond to more recent things first and earlier content later. In that space, I make sure that everyone is "touched" regularly—that is to say, that their thoughts and discussions are always acknowledged in some way. In the beginning, I remind everyone that if they're silent, it's as if they are not present, because no one can see them smiling or nodding their head. So to say something is a courtesy and it establishes one's presence. "To scream," I earnestly joke, "is a kindness."

As I led more and more email courses and seminars, I was astonished by what the participants wrote in their evaluations. Over and over the sighted students said the class was the best "online" learning experience they've ever had. At first I thought it was because I'm such an amazing teacher! But there's something else going on. Here's how Mara Mills, a professor of media studies at New York University, described her experience with one of my seminars: "Minimalist in design, lavish in ideas; I learned *so much*. Unexpected to me was how engaged I felt the whole time." Michele Friedner, professor of anthropology at the University of Chicago, had a similar reaction, writing:

> What I found was that while . . . Clark's class was incredibly pared down, bare bones perhaps, there was rich opportunity within the structure of the course to connect with others and that the seemingly minimal affordances of text only led to the creation of new kinds of contact, touching, and close engagement.

The texture of virtual touch they found in my email classes was novel to them, but it is ancient in our community. In their previous experiences with fancy online stuff, they may have been logged in and in extensive contact with the materials, their peers, and the instructors, but how did it feel? Apparently many of those encounters are abrasive and fatiguing. They are abrasive and fatiguing because institutions strive to have their online offerings replicate what was already abrasive and fatiguing: white, neurotypical, and distantist pedagogy.

The seminar I offer most frequently is "Introduction to Protactile Theory." That has made people smile. Teaching about Protactile language and practices—built around touch—via English, in text only, and by email alone? How contradictory! But the ground whence Protactile sprang is the same ground that has allowed us, for over one hundred and seventy years, to connect and connect and connect. By any means. We connect in spite of distantism. Sighted and hearing people are distantist in spite of having no shortage of means to connect. The artist and philosopher Erin Manning recently warned that the great danger in our society's response to COVID-19 is that

. . . it packs us into a tidy separateness. This tidy separateness is not a shared resource. It is only available to those who already benefited from distantism. It is only for those who are already at a distance, who already gain from individualism's one-upmanship.

In feeling our way forward, I think of a quote by good old Kurt Vonnegut. "Human beings will be happier," he wrote, "not when they cure cancer or get to Mars, but when they find ways to inhabit primitive communities again." Through accidents of history and by necessity, our community has always nurtured the fellow feelings of a family and the vibrations of a village. It has to do with scale. One thing that makes Protactile unique among all the languages of the world is that you cannot speak Protactile while physically alone. Another person's body—with their trust and sharing in producing speech—is required. We touch each other to speak. One also cannot address millions at once, holding forth from a stage. In our virtual spaces—via letter-writing and email—one can address any number of people, but the email groups that give the most life are powerfully small.

TACTILE ART

I

Downtown Saint Paul is home to one of the most extensive skyway systems in the world. The sprawling maze connects buildings via enclosed bridges above the streets. The skyway solves one of our challenges as DeafBlind people traveling through a city: crossing busy intersections. My family lived there for as long as we could afford to because it was such a joy to be a mouse racing inside and out, up and down, plying my long single whisker. Following my nose, I found all the best places to eat and, following other instincts, I infiltrated all the cleanest bathrooms hidden away from the masses.

One day my partner, Adrean, an ASL Deaf artist, came home to tell me about something she'd spotted. It was a sculpture of a giant open Braille book. She had never gone that way before, but I'd passed by it several times. It stood in a building's courtyard, some paces from the street. You had to see it to see it.

A few days later friends from out of town were visiting. We took them out to our beloved Ruam Mit Thai, and after our feast we gave them a tour of the city. I remembered Adrean's sighting and asked her to show us the public work.

It turned out to be a huge sheet of metal propped up, its bottom edge near the ground and its top edge a foot taller than I. Each Braille dot was the size of a golf ball. This made it impossible to read the text, which was supposed to be a passage from a Walt Whitman poem. Although the sheet mimicked the open face of a book, with two facing pages, each line ran across both pages.

There was a plaque with the title, artist name, perhaps a statement. Did the statement pay tribute to Braille? This information was not available in regular Braille.

As I struggled to read what the golf balls had to say, a security guard trundled out of the building. He spoke no sign language but we got the message. One of the nice secret restrooms was close by, and we hurried there to wash our hands.

II

Museums are difficult to get to. They don't want me to touch anything. They require that I make an appointment—by phone, no less. So my information about mainstream aesthetics has largely come from ducks.

They rule over gift shops, Goodwills, and garage sales. Squeaking rubber versions have long been infants' first encounter with artifice. Minnesota's state bird is the loon, and many homes and stores here feature wooden, ceramic, metal, stone, plush, and glass loons. Waterfowl are a favorite of woodcarvers. There is even a DeafBlind Canadian who whittles, paints,

and sells ducklings. What they all have in common is a flat
bottom. A goodly portion of their natural anatomy is taboo.
They are meant to appear floating on the still waters of a table-
top, a windowsill, or a bookshelf.

The hitch is that were I to handle a live duck paddling
across a pond, I would be able to feel it as a whole, for water is
not a tactile barrier as it is a visual one.

Small wonder, then, that one of my definitions of beauty
is a certain stuffed wood duck in the nature center at Rich-
field, Minnesota. A piece of ordinary taxidermy, its feathers
are ridiculously soft. "Wood Duck," I was inspired to write in
a slateku, a form I invented using the Braille slate, "I feel for
you / You never had hands to stroke / Your own wings." Even
more bewildering are its round velvet bottom and granular
webbed feet, which bespeak a master creator.

III

"Here, you can touch my face."

"Thank you, no."

"No, it's fine. Really."

"Nah. I just—"

"I want you to."

Well, I want to tell them, what you are offering for my
inspection is just a skin-covered skull.

"A head," jokes the eighteenth-century British comedian
George Alexander Stevens, "is a mere *bulbous excrescence*,
growing out from between the shoulders like a wen; it is
supposed to be a mere expletive, just to wear a hat on, to fill
up the hollow of a wig, to take snuff with, or have your hair
dressed upon."

A friend once showed me a prized possession of his, an egg-shaped sculpture. I could feel its eyebrows, nose, and mouth, but they conveyed nothing. For my sighted friend, it had an exquisite expression of serenity. "Peace," it's called.

At least it was bald. The bust of Mark Twain in a museum I visited in New York had him wearing a futuristic helmet, with fantastical whorling grooves. A terrible tumor grew under his nose. Ulysses S. Grant was similarly helmeted but had an iceberg stuck up his jaw.

Helmets notwithstanding, sculptors were on to something with nudity and gesture until the Victorians began to manufacture a statue for every philanthropist and politician. Of these "leaden dolls," G. K. Chesterton, the early-twentieth-century British writer and social critic, grouses, "Each of them is cased in a cylindrical frock-coat, and each carries either a scroll or a dubious-looking garment over the arm that might be either a bathing-towel or a light great-coat."

IV

CUBIST STATUE
after Jacques Lipchitz's "Matador," 1915

You are the best one
in the museum. You don't
try to be real. You
are wise not to attempt
hair. You have no face.
Your clothes make you. You
were inspired by a youth
famous for pretending to be

a statue. He would die
five years later. But you
are still here. We touch
you. You do not flinch.

V

We will call her Allie. Shortly after her death I learned from friends that she was a fake. It was one reason she had relocated some years earlier, to leave a local DeafBlind community that had caught on to her.

I had known—or, rather, not quite known—Allie for many years as a fellow member on multiple listservs in our community. I'd met her in the flesh only once. The posthumous revelations were not that shocking; we've always had DeafBlind wannabes or compulsive sympathizers in our midst. For better or for worse, they are part of our lives. Whatever it is that any of them gets out of it, many do give of themselves in return.

In Allie's particular case, she also gave me the most tactile work of art I own. It is a marvelous mosaic of seashells, judiciously arranged so as to have it rise and fall by turns from roaring densities to quieter rumblings. Though just two inches at its tallest point, it is a work of such soaring lyricism that I begin to understand what is meant by the sublime.

A long-distance DeafBlind friend of Allie's had lovingly put it together for her. It was the first time the artist had made something with a fellow DeafBlind person in mind. Allie explained to me that, unfortunately, the artist's other work is visual, primarily concerned with color, with only feeble tactile features. Like many blind and DeafBlind artists, Allie's friend catered to sighted customers and believed she knew what they wanted.

So it was a DeafBlind fake who had challenged a real DeafBlind person to make an intentionally tactile piece for the first time.

I cannot stop running my hands over it. When Allie knew she was going to die, she sent it with a note saying, "This piece cried out to be enjoyed by Mr. Tactile so it goes to you. Love, Allie."

VI

When I attended Deaf school growing up, I learned about a sickness that infects many hearing people. It keeps them awake at night unless they do something to bring music into our supposedly silent world. Dance troupes, bands, orchestras, and ex-hippie sound engineers invaded our campus every year.

I would later learn that sighted people were often afflicted in the same way. Only their desperate mission is to make visual art accessible to blind people. One victim of this malady is John Olson, a photojournalist and war photographer who made his mark dispatching images from the wars in Vietnam. After an illustrious career spanning five decades, he found himself wondering "what it was like for those who didn't have access to art, to photography. I wondered what it was like for the blind community, who couldn't access visual information. It was at that moment, on a Labor Day weekend of 2008, that I set out to develop a means by which blind people could see art, could see photographs, and could acquire visual information."

For the past fourteen or so years, he has been busy with his company 3DPhotoWorks, creating raised representations of art, photography, maps, and graphics. As he told a convention of the National Federation of the Blind in July 2018, "it has been my goal from the very beginning to create a worldwide network of museums, science centers, libraries, and institutions willing to provide the world's blind population with visual information using this tactile medium."

No one seems to have asked whether we want access to visual information. Why would we want a representation of a representation of something? Why not a tactile representation of that something, bypassing visual representation altogether? Why force visual art to be what it is not? We accept that most visual art is meant to be visual alone. Sighted people and institutions are the ones having trouble reconciling themselves to this fact.

VII

What shall we call it—tactile grammar, semiotics of touch, Protactile aesthetics, tactiletics? True tactile art must have language. It should express and extract meaning. Texture, contour, temperature, density, give, recoil, adsorption, and many other elements are units in this language.

Most things made by sighted people that we touch fail to make sense. Heft is one common grammatical unit they get wrong.

There are many toy tanks, for example, that replicate the shape and many of the moving parts of a real tank. Visually, it looks exactly like the real thing, and is thus able to exude some of its menace.

In the tactile realm the toy tank is a joke, because it is made of flimsy plastic parts and is light, being hollow and without ballast. If I wished to install an exhibit about the terrors of totalitarianism, tanks rolling over protesters like so much cardboard, I would need tanks with real heft. The protesters can be made of, well, cardboard, and can even be taller than the tanks. But the power is with the heft, and the tanks have it.

Or if I wanted to send a more hopeful message, I could reverse things. The tanks are made of cardboard, while the protesters possess the gravity of rock. The tanks could be much bigger, but the power, again, is with the heft. Visually, the power is with size; tactilely, size is much less important. That's grammar.

VIII

One winter, not long ago, your parents invite you and your boys to join them at the Minnesota Landscape Arboretum to visit its greenhouse. It is lovely to inhale the heavy air, which makes your lungs giddy. Smiling, you reach out—

Cacti.

So much for unfettered intercourse with nature.

As you tiptoe deeper into the garden, you find where the proper plants are and begin to examine them. There, among the pencil trees and ferns, you meet the most beautiful flowering plant.

It has a fan of smooth arching blades, and from the fist that holds this fan sprout stems stretching out at odd angles. A matte-like human skin covers these stems, and it reminds you of a warm handshake.

Excited, you look for someone to read the label, because nothing is in Braille here. The first sighted person you find is your mother. You tug her to meet your new friend and you ask her its name. She looks and says there is no label. "Why," she then inquires of you, "do you want to know the name of such an ugly plant?"

Taken aback, your mind slips inside its library and pulls out Mary Shelley's 1818 novel *Frankenstein*. It is the story of a tall, loose-limbed gentleman who had been assembled in a laboratory. When he emerged into the world, however, he could find no one willing to be his friend—except for a blind man. They were engaged in a productive conversation when the blind man's sighted family returned from their outing. Seeing the tall gentleman, they screamed.

Poor fellow, so unjustly treated! Well, you would be this plant's friend. You decide that its name is "Frankenstein's Handshake."

IX

We have DeafBlind artists, but do we have DeafBlind art?

The potters carefully glaze for visual effect. Legos are easy to build with, but are hideous to the touch. Many attend painting and drawing classes at centers for the blind. There are dancers who spin into empty air. Actors hope they are aimed in the right direction. Hundreds have beaded or woven or quilted tapestries that are tactilely blank. Artists ask sighted assistants "What color is this?" and "Does it look all right?"

Sir Joshua Reynolds, the eighteenth-century Deaf British portraitist, provides a crude but helpful formula. "The regular progress of cultivated life," he wrote, "is from necessaries to accommodations, from accommodations to ornaments." We don't have all our necessaries in place as tactile people. As yet we own very little of the material world and are forced to make do with sighted things.

But it isn't true that we haven't made much art. We have an incredibly rich literature. We probably have more writers per capita than any other community in the world. It is because there is one space within which we have gone from necessity all the way to art: our traditional virtual space. Our correspondence networks and access to books began in the middle of the nineteenth century and have served as our home until we could begin to make claims on the corporeal world.

The goal of the Protactile movement is for us to get, do, and make everything in our own way. After we peeled our language away from visual sign language and remade it completely, reciprocally, and proprioceptively tactile, Protactile storytelling, Protactile poetry, and Protactile theatre quickly emerged. It makes sense that those forms came first, as they don't require that we buy anything or lug equipment around or hammer something together. Just ourselves and each other. Protactile theatre, though, is starting to play with costumes and props. Does this mean Protactile art is next?

X

I once dreamed about installing an exhibition of assemblage art, using familiar objects that my friends would recognize immediately. The only glue I use is gravity. They can lift anything, handle it in their hands.

Some of the pieces were:

A 1970s cassette player with the slot popped open. Inserted within is a sticky toy wind-up brain that pulsates. "The Brain Implant."

A Midwestern-sized cereal bowl filled with hearing-aid earmolds. Silver spoon. "Breakfast of Champions."

A coffin made of old and used white folding canes. At rest inside, surrounded by a few lilies, is a wrecked Franklin Mint replica of a car. "Accident."

In another dream the exhibit is called "Buried Treasures." Each box is filled with a hand-sinkable substance—sawdust, popcorn, glass beads, and, my favorite, quinoa. Buried inside these boxes are surprise objects that juxtapose with the materials we dig through to get at them.

In another dream, a museum has lovely railings that take us from one exhibit to another, following the poetry of co-navigation. But another dream shoves it aside because the museum is now a gloriously walled labyrinth. It leads into a burrowing tunnel. This, in turn, cedes to a dream of water.

In another dream, I meet Genghis Khan. Most DeafBlind people have Usher syndrome, whose genetic history can be traced back to the Mongolian juggernaut. I realize from this wonderful statue in the dream that wood is so suggestive of living flesh; that most statues should be naked and then covered with clothing or representations thereof, for we feel right through clothes in real life; and that foam is a fine way to represent hair. Beneath his armor and linens I could feel Genghis Khan's love handles and the loins whence we came.

In another dream I am in a vast library of tactile objects. Millions of objects are housed there. They have an acquisitions department and a replica-making department. Things too small to feel with my hands are magnified. Things too large to grasp are reduced to the right scale for manual inspection. Many of the library's holdings are real objects. Most importantly, the great bulk of the collection is mailable. I can order anything, and a few days later, a box arrives.

XI

Since most of what may be understood as tactile art doesn't exist yet, there are no master strokes. But this doesn't mean there haven't been lucky strokes. My friend Robert Sirvage, a DeafBlind architect and design consultant, stumbled upon two such examples while traveling in Norway in the fall of 2017.

Norway had then recently legislated the separation of church and state. The formerly official national Lutheran Church had seven Deaf churches—called Døvekirken—that provided many services to the Deaf and DeafBlind communities. Now that these churches would no longer administer these programs, the seven Døvekirken realized that they needed to reinvent themselves. Robert was hired to help them reimagine their role and their spaces.

As Robert was entering the Bergen Døvekirke, his cane rapped against the base of the first of two extraordinary works. A priest at the Døvekirke in Stavanger named Georg Abelsnes had created them with DeafBlind parishioners in mind. He gave the pieces to the new Døvekirke in Bergen when it opened its doors on December 10, 1989.

The first piece, *God Bless You*, rests on a board about three feet from the floor. The main portion is a sectional cut of a tree trunk, a section where it starts to spread its roots. The grains are pleasantly rough, and the middle grain is studded with gemstones.

Robert found himself moving his hands downward and outward, his thumbs bumping across or wiggling past the gemstones. He turned to ask his host how they said "bless" in Norwegian Sign Language. It was as he thought—the piece indeed invites hands to follow its grains and in doing so say the word "bless."

By returning to the top, this time beginning with closed fists, he discovered that the piece has another feature. Cleverly placed along its downward planes is a stick. When Robert moved his hands downward, he felt the stick gently opening up his hands. He marveled and later told his friends that the artwork is "all about motion and tempo, not static at all."

As wonderfully interactive as this piece is, nothing could have prepared Robert for what he encountered next. He was later given to understand that the second piece is called something like "God Loves and Protects You." Standing about four feet tall, it is made of rounded, polished, and unevenly-shaped wood. It has subtle suggestions of a head, neck, and torso. Just below and in front of the torso-trunk of the figure, the wood becomes hollow, and within this is another piece of wood with a different texture. It includes a handle carved to slide into one's grasp.

His host suggested that Robert walk around to hug the figure from behind. When he rested his head on the crook of the figure's neck, he told me, "My heart jumped. Holy— Remembering that I was in a house of worship stopped me from completing the thought. It felt like I was transgressing big here, but in a good way. It felt like I had found a whole new way of knowing God."

What he had done was to temporarily assume the place of God, leaning over to hug the figure, which could represent anyone Robert thought of God as holding or could even represent Robert himself, Robert as God embracing the figure as Robert, his hand the Hand of God holding the handle, perhaps the hilt of a sheathed sword.

Shaken, Robert stepped back to ask his host more about this "performative artwork." He learned that the DeafBlind parishioners and many others, upon entering, communed with both pieces, going through the whole motions of simultaneously performing and receiving the messages.

"After my host became distracted talking with someone else," Robert went on to share,

> I turned back to interact with it again. This time I let myself relax and hug the figure. To make the message clearer, I allowed my heart and physical being to radiate with tenderness and love. After a while, I stood up and caressed my body. Somehow I knew that I would retrieve myself if I said something, and I was instantly retrieved when I whispered, "Thank you."

NO STAGE

PART ONE: APRIL 2015

The other day I asked my Braille student at the beginning of our session how she was doing. She said she was still fuming over what had happened the previous evening at her church. Once a month her church hosts a DeafBlind group service, with plenty of volunteer tactile interpreters. On this particular occasion, the Deaf pastor thought he was presenting a treat: a performance by a touring Deaf Christian theatre company. As soon as my student mentioned "play," I squeezed her hand to signal a gasp, and said, "Say no more, say no more."

"Right, that," she said. "Afterward, we were gritting our teeth and had our claws out!"

We shared a moment of perfect sympathy before agreeing that the pastor meant well and didn't know how much we hate theatre.

That is, traditional theatre, the kind that involves multiple characters performing on a stage. A one-person show might be OK; certain kinds of ASL poetry and storytelling manage to carry over a bit through interpreters. But there's nothing more alien than a play on a stage. Sighted Deaf people love Deaf theatre, of course. Some, though not many, enjoy ASL-interpreted performances—they can view the hearing actors and stage sets. They can see an actor whip out a gun in anger and see from the interpreter why. Hearing blind people may derive pleasure from listening to the dialogue while receiving audio description. They'd hear the actor yell, "You stole my money!" and know from the description that a gun has now come into play. For DeafBlind people, there is no direct connection. It all comes through an interpreter, secondhand, in a jumble, and we're lost.

Is it any accident that the worst thing that's ever happened to our community is a play, William Gibson's *The Miracle Worker*? Not only does it portray the young Helen Keller as a savage, thus gratifying the public's need for monsters and their eventual taming, the play is most responsible for extending Helen's problematic legacy to such a point that her name is a stand-in for the entire global DeafBlind population.

Another social reason for distrusting traditional theatre is that we ourselves have been put on display ever since Samuel Gridley Howe pushed his pupil Laura Bridgman to perform her tongue-aided needlework every Saturday in front of gawking crowds. And often when we find ourselves on the stage, presenting or sitting on a panel, we don't have access to the event itself before or after doing our bit.

One picture of how deeply wrong mainstream public performance customs are for us comes from Jack Clemo, a Deaf-Blind Cornish poet. On his wedding day, he was led to the altar and waited until someone tapped him on the shoulder before uttering his vows. He did not know what the minister was saying and did not directly receive his hearing-sighted bride's vows. He was there, but was he part of his own wedding? While DeafBlind events (such as weddings) are much better and inclusive today, and the Protactile movement has given DeafBlind presenters unprecedented access to audience feedback, Jack's experience still serves as a thumbnail of what theatre means to both DeafBlind people on display and those who are in attendance. We're there, but are we part of it?

So I propose that true Protactile theatre is, first of all, for a DeafBlind audience and is not meant to be viewed from a distance. It means we get rid of the stage. No rows of chairs. And it must be theatre where we can be directors, actors—all personnel. Hearing and sighted people who can speak Protactile can be involved or attend, but my point is that no part of it would be out of our reach.

My thoughts on what Protactile theatre might be began to form in 2008 when I attended Louisiana Acadiana Deaf-Blind Citizens' annual April crawfish dinner fund-raiser. The event featured a DeafBlind clown from Georgia named Mark Gasaway, who, as it happens, is the current president of the American Association of the DeafBlind. He was the ILLY Clown, "ILLY" being a spin on the classic I Love You handshape and short for "I Love Loving You." He did what hearing-sighted clowns often do: mingle. In this context, it made something click in my head. Of course! Take the act to everyone.

He dressed in an outlandish and a very tactile costume, with huge boots and a hat with a ski jump for its bill. He went around teasing and playing pranks on everyone, showing them things from his many pockets. We felt him making balloon animals and swords and hats. He had a dog puppet in one hand, and we felt his other hand scolding it and the dog tucking in his head, begging forgiveness. He made contact with every person there at least twice.

Soon after that memorable weekend in the heart of Cajun country—which could be said to be DeafBlind country too, since Louisiana has the largest DeafBlind population in the United States—Seattle's DeafBlind Service Center hosted a fashion show in partnership with a local boutique, the Fashion Bug. Instead of having a runway, they had a banquet. The models, some of them DeafBlind, approached everyone. They interacted with each patron, showed off their outfits, pointed out interesting features, and often engaged in discussions about the fabric and prices. The staff from the Fashion Bug also matched each patron with an accessory or a hat to take home. They may not have realized it then, but something historic was happening.

These two events suggested to my mind one kind of play— the Mingle. What we have is a social event and we let everyone eat and have a good time while a play unfolds in our midst. The actors are like out-of-state visitors or, if they're historical characters, they are like they've just been dropped off by a time machine. The actors' task is to build the same basic story in the minds of everyone they meet. They have a set of messages to get across while working the room. Say you have a love-triangle story. We get to meet all three parties, listen to them rationalize or wax lyrical or bad-mouth another party. We get conflicting stories. We are asked what we think, to take sides, to give advice, even to intervene. "If you see Jean, tell her I never did it!" I'm sure we'll gossip with our fellow attendees in between our turns with the actors. There could be all sorts of formats. For example, there could be three very brief acts, which may mean the actors each do three rounds, while the attendees experience nine interactions with the story as it mounts toward its climax.

I think it's important to note here that we attendees would know that there's a play, and that Bill, Jean, and poor Luke are not real people. Theatre should never be about fooling people completely. There needs to be an element of cooperation from the audience, where the audience can choose to be drawn into the experience. Isn't theatre an instrument of self-deception on the part of the captivated? Yes, collusion is the key to illusion.

However, we do need assistance in fooling ourselves. But traditional theatrical illusion is very visual and almost never holds up to touch. I remember being invited backstage one time to feel the props. The experience was underwhelming. Everything felt worse than fake. I couldn't tell what half of the things were supposed to be. Take a knight's suit of chain mail. It was a piece of cloth with glitter painted on it. The costumes and props used in Protactile theatre would need to be tactilely appropriate. The chain mail doesn't have to come from the British Museum's Second Crusade collection, but it better be chain mail!

When the Protactile movement blossomed, I was thrilled with the possibilities it added to my dreams of what theatre could be. There are now presentations, workshops, and staff meetings being conducted without interpreters, following patterns of small group discussions and rotating people around so that everyone gets the same information directly. In spring 2014, Gallaudet University had two classes that were done in this way, without the traditional setup of a professor lecturing in front of students.

The Mingle is not the only model for Protactile theatre. Another is a series of monologues, which do occur in traditional theatre. Only there would be a room with the actors arranged around the room, ideally sitting on chairs with two chairs near each one of them. Protactile allows for speakers to "double" what we're saying by having both hands function as dominant hands. Thus, two listeners can take in the message at the same time. If the order of interactive monologues isn't essential, attendees can go ahead and sit with all of the performers and rotate from there. If the order is important, then there is a queue.

That's the bare-bones version. But this template can be built on in any number of ways. For example, there can be parts where, instead of having two listeners following a single actor, an attendee can take in two actors talking to each other or having a fight or romancing each other. There can be acts. Act One, attendees go into the room in turn, come out and socialize until Act Two opens, and they go in there again to find out what happens next. You can go anywhere with the costumes and props, from minimalist to elaborate. Unlike the Mingle, the theatre room allows for more complex productions, such as Shakespeare adapted to suit a fixed number of turns around the room.

If I could have my dream play become a reality, as it were, I'd like it to extend beyond just one room. Why not a house, especially an old house? If it's a murder play, we attendees would be arriving at the house as if we were the detective. We meet the cop first, who briefs us on the crime scene. With our cop as our partner, ready to ask the right questions or offer speculations if our own faculties fail us, we meet the weeping father, and then the mother, who is cooler. We inspect the corpse, which is still warm, and we ignore the fact it's still breathing. We handle the murder weapon, which isn't made of cardboard. During the intermission in the dining room, while we're enjoying refreshments and debating which suspect killed the cook, there's a crash and the plot thickens. As we interview the suspects a second time, it dawns on us who did it.

In other words, my dream play would make me part of it. The wily playwright would decide who the audience is to be, and the audience, who is I, would suddenly become an actor.

PART TWO: APRIL 2020

In five years, Protactile has evolved so far and so fast! The first Protactile theatre production took place on October 20, 2017, in the basement of Jelica and Vince Nuccio's home in Seattle. Jelica had for some time been running a training center, Tactile Communications, out of her home, and two of her students had chosen to adapt O. Henry's classic short story "The Gift of the Magi" for their final project.

After the success of their project, Yashaira Romilus and Jasper Norman quickly founded Protactile Theatre, a grassroots touring resource that partners with local DeafBlind communities to produce plays. To date, there have been nine productions, going from coast to coast, from Seattle to Austin to Washington, D.C., to Los Angeles. All nine plays have come alive in private homes.

When my dreams of our own theatre were first published, they inspired an English professor at Gallaudet University named Jill Bradbury to apply for a National Endowment for the Arts grant. Her application proposed a brief institute to work on a Protactile adaptation of *Romeo and Juliet*. Upon winning the grant, Jill hired me to develop a variety of models. But when the DeafBlind participants learned that Gallaudet intended to hold the two-week institute on campus, we protested. In an open letter to the university president dated February 6, 2018, I explained that

> Gallaudet is one of the most hostile and inaccessible environments I've ever encountered. To mention just a few things: Everything and everyone is spread over considerable distances, making the campus the very definition of distantism. There are vast seas of concrete with few or no tactile and natural landmarks. Even so basic a task as getting food can be incredibly difficult, where there are no accessible menus, no Braille labels or tactile markings, and staff are behind counters and glass with no openings for tactile communication.

Gallaudet eventually agreed to have the workshop moved to Jelica and Vince Nuccio's home in Seattle. At the time, there had only been two productions, and this workshop constituted the third, in August 2018. Already it was becoming a pattern: We worked and played best in the warm and intimate spaces of a house. Indeed, most institutional buildings, especially those in the modernist and brutalist molds—with hospital-smooth floors, sterile air, hard surfaces, sharp corners, and depressingly open spaces—tend to silence Protactile bodies. For the purposes of theatre, the affordances of a home are even more important, offering a wealth of walls, small rooms in which to bounce around, and bumpable furniture. A house where people *live* lends itself wonderfully to magic-making.

One of my favorite stories about the early days of Protactile theatre concerns a DeafBlind girl who is a wheelchair user. Her mother had somehow gotten wind of the Austin production of "The Gift of the Magi" and decided to buy tickets. To understand the significance of her decision, you need to know that there is very little contact between our community and DeafBlind children, whose education is in the hands of hearing-sighted people historically unwilling to include us in the field of education. The ideological message to parents of DeafBlind children is clear: Keep away from DeafBlind adults, because you don't want your child to grow up to be like them. But this mother was able to put that aside and take what must have felt like a leap into the unknown.

When Yashaira and Jasper realized that they had a patron in a wheelchair, they adapted their choreography on the spot and whisked the girl, with mother in tow, into the world of the play. The girl felt everything. She gasped when she and the wife together felt the wife's freshly shorn hair.

A few weeks later Yashaira received an email from the mother begging Protactile Theatre to come back. Her daughter had been playing out parts of the play every single day. It was driving the mother bonkers, but then she realized that her daughter never had before obsessed over a TV show or a celebrity. Now she had a hero: Yashaira Romilus.

Recently I asked Yashaira how much it would cost to have her come to Minnesota and help whip together a Protactile play. "Any amount," she said. "It can be very cheap. I'm willing to sleep on a couch." She launched into a rundown of things we would need. "We strongly prefer that we use a DeafBlind person's house, but if that's not possible, then someone's house, a friend's or an ally's. And teamwork is a *must*. We'll need two DeafBlind people to join the cast. It doesn't matter what their level of Protactile fluency is. We'll make it work. Two Deaf-Blind volunteers to lead the reception area, cooking and serving food, and . . ." All of the details are designed to promote our sense of community, agency, and ownership.

One common misconception about Protactile theatre is

that it's experimental theatre. Many hearing and sighted people who first learn about it immediately bring up plays they've been to or heard of that "break the fourth wall." Such plays are interactive, planting actors in the audience or inviting audiences to mingle with the actors. But Protactile theatre itself is not experimental. How do hearing and sighted people do an old-fashioned high school Shakespeare play in Elizabethan costumes? They do it on a stage in front of a large audience. How would we do the same? Well, we do it in a house, with actors interacting directly with patrons. Our default isn't about breaking a fourth wall, because we were never within those walls on a stage to begin with. In fact, Protactile theatre has built up the traditionally invisible fourth wall, cutting off any large audience from viewing anything from a distance.

This isn't to say that we don't experiment. We are always experimenting! Someday some of us will turn avant-garde within Protactile theatre, where we start doing really conceptual work or performance art or breaking whatever borders emerge in traditional Protactile theatre. For now, we are thrilled to put on skits and informal takes on classic plays. The latest major development is *A Christmas Carol*, the first play to combine two models I drafted for the *Romeo and Juliet* workshop: the Conveyor Belt and You Are.

Up to that time, most of the Protactile plays took in one to three patrons at a time for the whole play. Patrons were told to arrive at different times close to their turns to enter the play. The Conveyor Belt, by contrast, sets out a series of scenes in different areas or rooms. Each one might have its character or characters. The first patron connects with the first scene and then passes on to the second scene. The first scene is then made available for the next patron. If a play has four scenes, it may mean that there are four patrons being engaged at any given time, until the last one brings up the tail end of the process and we call it a night. There are a few tricks for handling how patrons are passed and how to keep a patron engaged for longer when the next scene is taking more time. Different patrons may have different communication styles and ways of relating to the content, so the elasticity is essential. Protactile performers do not follow scripts line by line, but must constantly adjust how they convey the story.

In the first few plays, there was one DeafBlind patron at a time, fully immersed, communing with the actors in Protactile. Meanwhile, there was often a sighted patron or two tagging along, experiencing the play partly tactilely and partly visually, eavesdropping on the Protactile dialogue with their hands on the DeafBlind patron. Many sighted patrons expressed a wish that they could have been fully immersed as well. The Conveyor Belt innovation allows a play to plunge all patrons into Protactile without it meaning only one person is in there for the whole play at a time. While no play has yet imposed a rule that sighted patrons be blindfolded, many sighted patrons have opted to go blindfolded. This is an excellent choice, because none of the props consider visual appearance.

You Are is an approach where the patron functions as a character in the play, sort of like how second-person narratives work. Related to this feature is our growing penchant in Protactile pedagogy for role playing. Many of the workshops at the first intensively Protactile conference, Northwest DeafBlind Conference in March 2018, utilized role-playing. For their revolutionary workshop on racism, Yashaira, Oscar Chacon, and Korian Thomas assigned different roles to participants and had us act out scenes and debrief afterward. "You are me chilling in the store, waiting for my friend to meet me there. You are the police officer who accosted me. And you're the store owner who tried to intervene. Ready? Go!"

Victoria Magliocchino, a leader of the Florida DeafBlind Association and a brilliant DeafBlind writer, first learned about the Conveyor Belt and You Are mechanisms through the *Romeo and Juliet* workshop. When she and Yashaira decided to put on something because it was nearing Christmas, Vicky was inspired to write our most sophisticated adaptation to date. It premiered on December 14, 2019, in what we call the Barn, the Nuccios' new home in Monmouth, Oregon, a few blocks from the Protactile House, where Tactile Communications is headquartered. It was my joy to attend as a mere patron.

I was scheduled to go in last, but I went to the Barn hours ahead to hang out. There I had the pleasure of meeting a Deaf-Blind child whose family had decided to dive into our forbidden world. Tea, cookies, and finger foods were served. A dear friend named Clamp and Shake and I talked theory. When the King—my esteemed colleague in the Protactile movement—came out of the play gushing, he stopped himself: "I better say nothing and let you experience it for yourself!" My old boss, a DeafBlind administrator in the telecommunications industry, surprised me by showing up, having carpooled with friends from Seattle four hours away. I was delighted to learn that Darcie, a Deaf interpreter, had known the late Deaf Native American artist John L. Clarke, for whom I have a soft spot as a near namesake. Her father had taught the young Clarke art at the Montana School for the Deaf, and she owns several of Clarke's now priceless works, including a huge carved wood panel. I was about to secure a solemn promise to visit and feel those works when Jelica swooped in and seized me. It was my turn.

She first showed me her intricately beaded and embroidered

dress, which whispered of the Victorian age. "You are," she said, "a mean, hard-hearted old man named Ebenezer Scrooge. Your Protactile name is Bah Go Away, because that's what you always say. You've hurt so many people because of your selfishness, but tonight is your chance. Will you repent and have a change of heart? Here's your nightcap. Come follow me."

We went upstairs and into a bedroom, where my host tucked me into bed. It was quiet for a minute, then I felt thumping on the floor. Thump. Thump. Thump. Closer and closer. A shaking hand found me. "Are you Bah Go Away? Do you remember me?" The first ghost showed me the ball and chain clamped around their ankle. I was transported. One after the other, the ghosts indicted me and bade me feel the evidence of the harm I had inflicted, including a tiny nameless gravestone bearing only the carved letters "R.I.P." The play broke my heart and put it back together, for how could anyone, even Ebenezer Scrooge, resist?

MY DREAM HOUSE

Almost everything is built with hearing and sighted people in mind. DeafBlind people routinely come into conflict with features of architecture and design. And I do mean conflict— physical and sometimes violent conflict. So the first principle of DeafBlind Space is that it welcomes feeling bodies. Because most spaces are hostile to us, we've insisted on many rules being followed, such as leaving things in their places or returning them to their places. While those burdensome rules do help, they're by no means foolproof. The other day, for example, my wife opened an upper cabinet in the kitchen to take down some vitamins and was going to put the jar back up when—

So I'd like to focus on some ideas for what my dream house would be like if I could afford to have anything custom-made. The first thing is that it wouldn't be a house at all. I love skyways and living right in downtown, where I can hop on buses and subways or trains. But that's just me. I know many Deaf-Blind people who love living out in the country, enjoy farming or gardening, and who even hunt. So let's forget about whether it's a house and where it is on the map. What would be inside?

There would need to be a system of vibrating pads or plates as part of the flooring so that signals—for the door, for the Protactile phone (which doesn't exist yet, but I did say *anything*, didn't I?), smoke and fire, tornado and storm warnings—can reach me anywhere I may be within the premises. Geraldine Lawhorn, in her wonderful memoir *On Different Roads*, mentions an alternative: her use of fans. She and many of her contemporaries in the 1970s had rigged up fans to signaling devices. But it would just be one signal—the fans go off and you feel the air current changing, but what is it? Is it the door? Or the phone? What if I want the windows open? That's why I want vibrations—*bz bz bz* for the door, *buzzzzz* for the phone, and so on.

There are devices on the market that provide people with clip-on vibrating things or wristbands. But that breaks my number-two rule for what DeafBlind Space is: No tools or devices that I have to carry around with me. It may be OK and very smart to use a white cane out there in public, but if I have to use it at home, then it's not home. As imperfect as my present home is, my family and I have worked things out so I wouldn't need to use my cane. For example, we've declared certain routes in our home as freeways where we will not put a huge object in the way. DeafBlind Space means you don't need to carry anything. It means you can walk around naked, just like everyone does—well, at times.

One more thing about this system: It would be awesome if I could also stomp on the floor and get certain signals relayed to everyone else in my home. Each room could have its signature vibration, and everyone would know that someone was calling from a particular room. This reminds me of a true story: A famous DeafBlind couple, Leonard and Betty Dowdy, now gone to their rest, lived in Olathe, Kansas. Leonard liked to fix things around the place, and whenever Betty wanted to call him in, she'd open the kitchen window and spray out a rose fragrance. It didn't always work, or get him in quickly enough. One of these times it wasn't because he didn't smell it; it was because he was on the roof. How about adding these vibrating plates on the roof? No, that would be going too far. DeafBlind Space isn't meant to be accident-free or fail-safe. No space is. But our own kind of space gives us a different orientation, a different center of gravity.

One of the things that have caused much grief not just for DeafBlind people but for sighted Deaf people is how faucets are designed. Ask any DeafBlind or Deaf person, and they'll tell you it happened to them before—forgetting that the water was running until they notice the flood. Last year was my worst experience. It was the tub, and the water spilled over and seeped down to my neighbors' apartments both levels below us. Every time an accident happens, we get super-careful and remember, but then our grip loosens. What I have never understood is why those overflow holes in the tub or in the bathroom sink are never big enough to catch all the water. And kitchen sinks, except in old houses, never have a high enough ridge around or any overflow holes. There are actually various models available that would help some—foot-pedal, laser-eye automatic, etc. The reality, however, is that mass-produced designs assume hearing and sight.

Another enemy, one that has broken bone and shed blood, is the door. Closed doors are good doors, and open doors can often be good doors. But doors that are ajar or halfway open are *bad* doors. If a door doesn't really need to be there, don't have a door. If there needs to be a door, then it needs to be the kind that can be locked open or otherwise swing shut. I did wonder about sliding doors, but decided against them. Too easy to dislodge, too hard to reset or repair. (Note to everyone who likes to open doors for other people: Don't do it when you see a blind person. We are looking for a closed door, not an open one.)

Cabinets in the kitchen are somewhat different. Cabinet doors are good *only* when they're closed. They are bad in every other way. I haven't tested this, but maybe the best would be to have accordion-style folding panels, which would reduce the size of what juts out. Another approach might be roll-top design or cylindrical doors like the little ones in the fridge where you put butter in. It opens and its back moves inside the space.

Now I'm going to discuss something very particular and perhaps difficult for non-DeafBlind people to fully grasp, so bear with me as I try to explain it. You know the saying "Out of sight, out of mind"? Well, for DeafBlind people everything that's out of sight remains in the mind's eye. We can relate to what the painter Paul Gauguin once said: "I shut my eyes in order to see." This is why DeafBlind vision is often better than eyesight—we know where everything is and see through walls, through doors, through drawer, through anything in front of or under or above them. Nothing is hidden. The bad news is that we also see, or imagine that we see, everything that's behind the walls, under the fridge, inside the gap between the floor and the bottom of the cabinet under the sink.

We have been accused of being the spawn of the great Mr. Clean. But it's simply that we are aware of the dirt that's out of sight, dirt that sighted people would want to wipe out if it were visible. I wash the floor under the fridge every two weeks. I scrub the floor under the oven every two weeks. I wipe clean drawer grooves. I clean places that few sighted people ever think of. Recently, I went shopping for a new toaster. Feeling the long rows of toasters in various stores, I was aghast. My old one had a bottom flap that you could unlatch and have open out like a trapdoor. All of those new toaster models, every single one of them, had a locked bottom and only this little pan that you pull out to shake out the crumbs. I can promise you that there will be crumbs in there that the pan won't bring out and that turning the toaster upside down and shaking it won't liberate. I want the flap, because it facilitates thorough cleaning.

This situation gives you a glimpse of how differently a DeafBlind person can view "new" products that are supposedly better. We are alarmed by the massive move to make every single appliance digital, with a flat screen. Tactile knobs, buttons, and switches are fast disappearing from the marketplace. Increasingly, garage and estate sales are the places to go.

In the kitchen, where crumbs are apt to fall and where liquids pursue gravity, I want the lower parts of the kitchen—cabinets, fridge, oven, dishwasher, baseboards—to be redesigned in ways that would accommodate regular and vigorous cleaning. To take the cabinet under the sink as an example, I know that there are unidentified life forms under its bottom and behind the baseboard. I want to annihilate these. At first, I thought of just having no cabinet there at all. Just open space under the sink, just the floor there. But then I remembered that it's important for my foot to hit the baseboard under the kitchen sink first. Hitting, in the tactile realm, is good. It's sought-for contact, not conflict, when these things are landmarks.

Many times when I go out in public someone will try to help me avoid hitting a wall or a ledge, not realizing it was my goal to find these things. Having my foot making contact with certain parts of my home is similar to this, and I would want my foot to hit the baseboard under the kitchen sink, or my legs to pleasantly collide with the lower cabinet doors. If there were nothing there, then I'd have to hold out my hand to hit the counter. That would be a drag. In addition to not needing the cane and not carrying any devices, DeafBlind Space means you don't need to hold out your hands. It means you don't get hit in the shins or your vital organs don't get whammed because there was nothing to greet your foot first. It also means the place is friendly to shoulder-brushing and hip-ricocheting, among other natural contact-making movements. Bumpability is an essential quality.

So I would still have the cabinet under the kitchen, and I would still have the baseboard right under its bottom. What I want is for the bottom of the cabinet to open like a car hood. I would, from time to time, take out the dishwasher soap, the box of fresh trash bags, etc., and lift the bottom and clean the floor underneath and wipe out any mental eyesores I find there.

It's worth repeating that hitting is sought-for contact. Just as sighted people make "eye contact" with objects all the time as they move through space, turning here, pausing there, tuning out until they see a certain landmark, we DeafBlind people *want* to make contact with our environment. And we do. But some things were never made for such contact. We can, as I have done in my home and office, make traditional spaces to some degree contact-friendly. A constant and very real thorn in the side, though, is the corner.

Homes and workplaces harbor veritable armies of corners. Wall corners, table corners, partition corners, corners of cabinets, corners of opened drawers, corners of railings . . . Speaking broadly, corners can be good. I love inside corners. The problem is when an outside corner or edge is square and sharp. In DeafBlind Space, then, all of these would be rounded, all around. Turn a hallway and feel the wall curve around. Lean on a table and feel a convex pressure against your chest. Sit on the edge of the same table, and have it feel like sitting on someone's lap. Remember that we want to hit everything. It is crucial that what we hit be flat or blunt. Materials like rubber, leather, vinyl, fabric, various kinds of firm foam—those should be used liberally, too.

Regarding furniture, it's amazing what they say about a culture. Take the love seat. The way it's designed makes a clear picture of two people sitting side by side, looking at something, not each other. An expression of phonocentric culture if ever there was one. A Protactile love seat would be very different, having the two sitters face each other, thigh against thigh, almost hip to hip. To support three-way or four-way conversations, we'd have a nifty kind of plush chair that can be easily moved around. We'd also have nests. We wouldn't have the traditional big dining table, which moves everyone beyond tactile contact. Instead, food and people would switch places, with people on the inside and food outside. A U-shaped table can be used, so that everyone's food is either behind them or at their side, but not in the way of conversation. This also makes it much easier to serve food, without trying to move plates and cups through the forest of happy arms and hands. Restaurants hate us because we always screw up their floor plan.

Some of the foregoing may have suggested that it must be tough to be DeafBlind and live out there, suffering conflicts with hostile spaces. The reality is that we become master navigators and we can be very happy and comfortable with most everything. I gained a better understanding of this one morning many years ago. Every morning, I followed a routine that included reaching for the knob of a bathroom drawer. My fingers always landed on that knob without my ever looking for it. Pure autopilot. On this morning, however, I was made aware of something because, though my hand landed on the knob like always, it did so at a slightly different angle. Thinking about it for a second, I realized that I'd forgotten to put the rug back on the floor after washing it and hanging it to dry the previous day. So the rug had played a role in my daily morning routine, but only a tiny role. If it had played a bigger role, maybe I would've fumbled around a bit. Instead, its absence from its usual place on the floor hardly changed anything. Indeed, I've gone for that knob and hit it while holding a water bottle in one hand, or while consciously avoiding brushing my shoulders against the walls when they had fresh paint on them, or while talking with one of my kids and walking there at the same time.

While we do naturally mold our movements around the built environment we encounter, we can be asked to adapt too much. Distantism had trained us in the past to sail through space and to aim for our destinations along sighted people's routes. Protactile has helped us to abandon these performances, the stunts that make sighted people ask us, "How did you know where it is?" We have taken to patting along walls, to hopping among many more landmarks, to fumbling. It used to be that we needed order; now a mess is perfectly fine. But traditional spaces often do not facilitate those more relaxing and rewarding movements. So our movements will need to attack such spaces and open up new grooves.

PART FOUR

HOW IT
FEELS TO US

A FABLE

There was a certain king in this very Savatthi.
And that king addressed a man: "Come now, my good
man, bring together all those persons in Savatthi who
have been blind from birth."
"Yes, your majesty," that man replied, and
after detaining all the blind people in Savatthi, he
approached the king and said, "All the blind people in
Savatthi have been brought together, your majesty."
"Now, my man, show the blind people
an elephant."

—from "The Blind Men and the Elephant" in the
Tittha Sutta, translated from the Pali by John D. Ireland

The sun's warm breath found the six men in their usual places, playing their elaborate game of shifting and scooping up stones. Their hands slid over and under one another as stone clicked against stone. They spoke fast, in a rustling stream no sighted ear could catch.

Ridhan was the first to scent it. "We've got a visitor."

The five others paused to listen. Parth, the oldest among their company, said, "Who?"

"Don't you smell it? It's an elephant, I'm sure."

They sniffed the air. "How do you know it's an elephant?" Nehal prodded Ridhan in his side. "You've never seen one."

"I don't know how I know." Ridhan jumped up. "Let's go see."

"Wait," Parth said. "There's money in this."

Ridhan groaned.

"Sit back down, Ridhan," Parth commanded. "Let's wait and see if this means a show."

The others murmured their assent. Ridhan slapped his stick against the ground. "Do we have to? We've got enough money."

Parth shoved a sharp silence into their midst. The others held their breath.

Finally, Nehal quipped, "Maybe we'll get so much money, we'll buy ourselves an elephant!"

It took a while before the first sighted villager noticed the elephant. The men listened as the rumor of its presence spread. Calls of "Elephant! Elephant!" steered the inhabitants toward the southern well.

"I knew it was an elephant," Ridhan said.

"Yes," Parth grunted. "But not a word about it now. You all know what to do."

They resumed their game, or rather pretended to, for they were no longer keeping score.

After an interval, three sighted girls came running up. "Uncles! We've got something to show you!"

"Ah, you darlings," Parth crooned. "Tell us, tell us what it is."

"No, no, no," the girls squealed. "We won't tell!"

"Aw," Nehal said, "but we're busy. Do we really have to go?"

As the six men approached the elephant, the villagers began to cheer. Parth signaled with his stick for his companions to start tripping and bumping into one another. He led them on a course that veered away from the elephant.

One of the girls shouted, "Not there! Let me show you!" She grabbed Parth's hand and took him to the elephant's side.

Parth bowed toward the girl. "Thank you ever so much, beautiful one!"

The five other men clustered around Parth, their arms, shoulders, legs, garments, and backs taking in the elephant. Nehal exclaimed under his breath, "It's much smaller than I thought it would be. The way the legends go on so, you'd think—"

One of the others agreed. "What a dud."

Ridhan whispered, "It's beautiful."

"Shut up," Parth snapped. "Time to work. I'll stay here. Nehal, you take the front. Ridhan, go behind."

The six men spread themselves around the elephant.

The crowd shouted, "What is it? We don't know! Tell us!"

A young man in the back of the crowd yelled, "Of course we know what it is. You blind men, it's an elephant!"

The crowd turned and hissed. Parth quickly boomed, "So it is, so it is. But we have never touched an elephant before. Let me see what it is like!"

He patted the elephant's front left leg up and down.

"It's a pillar!" he sang out.

The crowd laughed. Parth smiled and bowed. "Some pennies, dear friends?"

Several coins flew toward him.

"Thank you, our beloved friends. Now we shall hear what my brethren in darkness make of the fabled elephant."

The man standing behind Parth began swinging the elephant's ear.

"You're wrong!" he sang out. "It's nothing like a pillar. It's like a huge fan!"

The crowd laughed and more coins flew.

"Oh no!" sang out another man. "It's like a wall!"

"You blind fools!" sang out another, who was caressing the elephant's trunk. "It's like a tree branch!"

"You know nothing, nothing, nothing!" sang out Nehal. He kissed the tip of a tusk, gripping it as it moved. "It's like a spear!"

There was a pause. Ridhan, standing behind the elephant, hadn't said anything.

The crowd murmured, "There's one more. You, what is it like?"

Ridhan sighed. "All of this is—"

Parth shot back a warning.

Ridhan drew himself to his full height and held up the elephant's twitching tail. In a flat voice, he said, "It's a rope."

READING ENVIRONMENTS

The National Library Service for the Blind and Print Disabled (NLS) has finally selected several good books of poetry. Most of their earlier selections had been duds. They emboss only a handful of poetry titles each year, because the majority of their patrons' fingers are hungry for romances, mysteries, and thrillers. Anxiously checking for updates, I felt frustrated that they had wasted yet another precious poetry pick. But now I had access to some truly wonderful works.

What transpired when those books arrived in the mail amazed me. I was delighted by the first few poems and then I stopped. One after the other, I dropped these books. It was a relief returning to Project Gutenberg, which is a vast online repository of books that are no longer under any copyright restrictions. Why am I able to spend whole days and weeks lapping up turgid eighteenth-century verse while I cannot bear the incisive lines of a contemporary master?

Environment has a lot to do with it. As a Braille reader, I do not have access to every book I might be interested in. So it is not possible to be as immersed in contemporary poetry as I am in poetries of the past that are freely available in the public domain. Can one have a favorite from among ten items, or does one need to devour hundreds before acquiring affinities?

Limited access does have its benefits and comforts. I read many things I never would have if I could read anything. But for some reason, the few books of poetry produced in Braille by the NLS do not constitute such an environment. Project Gutenberg does. It may have to do with numbers, a certain critical mass. A certain scope that is neither overwhelming nor too narrow.

In Chile, books cost more than they do anywhere else in the world. I don't know all the reasons why, but I understand that when Chileans travel, they often hit a series of bookstores. Here is how the author Julio Ramón Ribeyro describes his experience of nervously visiting these stores:

> I usually leave without buying anything, because right away, at the sight of all those books, my desire to possess extends not only to several possible books but to all books in existence. And if I do happen to buy a book, I leave without any kind of contentment, because its acquisition signifies not one book more but many books less.

The opening poems in those recent NLS collections at first excited me, but the more they spoke to my heart the more painful they became. They made me realize there are many more poems I would have cherished if only I could have gotten my hands on them. Such is the profound effect of arbitrary and partial access. Sometimes it is better to have nothing than to have too little. Access denied is quite different from a natural restriction, such as one's limited book-buying budget, or a local library not having every book in the world, or one being able to read only in a specific language.

Another natural process is self-regulation. It may have been overwhelming for Ribeyro to see all those affordable books on a trip elsewhere—it surely would be overwhelming for me were all books of poetry to suddenly become accessible—but given time and a growing trust in a new environment we will be able to self-regulate. We will find our own narrow and happily selfish paths through the forest.

For writers, perhaps it is essential that our reading paths indeed be narrow. After all, we are to write. Some of us write what is missing, so it is good that we do not read everything. It would silence us to know too much. Some of us lean on the tree trunks of literature. That, too, entails not reading everything. Either way, we who have no choice can still write; likely we are even compelled to write.

But what does this not having a choice mean for us as writers, as human beings? Is the search for reading environments that are small but not too small itself a form of writing, a pre-composing of our minds? Much of what is in our minds and much of what we claim to be our perspectives are gifted to us. Or imposed. Is there a difference between me and a poet who can read a thousand books of poetry? Which of us is experiencing more freedom?

While their haphazard poetry offerings are a torment, the NLS does provide another kind of reading environment, one I inhabit with great pleasure. They emboss a number of magazines, which, unlike their books, we do not need to return. Like print magazines, they are disposable. I receive *National Geographic*, *Rolling Stone*, *Harper's Magazine*, the Royal National Institute for the Blind's *Short Stories*, and a few others. And there is *Poetry* magazine. The editors choose everything, but the environment is congenial. It is not partial or arbitrary access, because it's curated. The context is not like a forest, but more like a garden, each magazine a bouquet. I don't have to read every item, I can throw them into the recycling bin. Those magazines are more than I can read on the john, or in the bathtub, or at the park, or on a plane. They are well matched, magazines and transitory states of mind.

It is no accident that, as a marginalized reader, it is only the marginal that I have access to. Shakespeare and Whitman and Yeats may be available, but they are also difficult to digest. I have not been permitted to be omnivorous. Instead, less-known poets are my fare. They go down better. Should access to books for blind and print-disabled readers expand, should our copyright laws be overhauled, would I be able to change my diet and, per the "you are what you eat" dictum, become a different writer?

In addition to vexation, I feel pride. There is a brutal integrity in all DeafBlind writing. Some of my forebears may have purred and pandered and peddled, but they all wrestled with their reading environments. My work would not be Deaf-Blind poetry if I had a hearing and sighted person's access to books. Even if all the books in the world became accessible, it would still be an environment unique to DeafBlind readers who read in Braille, without recourse to audio or to book cover images, authors' photos, illustrations, pictures, comics, or graphics. Right now, the DeafBlind environment means very little contemporary mainstream poetry. It means plenty of dead imperialists. It means sharing stories and poems and jokes with each other in our many email communities. It also means the mainstream does not have access to much of our literature, though it would be good to change that situation. I do seek to publish my work in mainstream venues, and I carry

out and champion what are the first efforts to translate Protactile literature into English. Readers outside of our community
do not need, and actually should not have, full access to our
voices and stories, and we do not need, and actually should
not have, full access to all the voices and stories in the world,
but mutual exchange and being present in each other's reading
environments can only nourish.

As I write this I can feel my environment shifting. It is a
living thing, stretching, contracting, intersecting, dividing,
sometimes withdrawing in disgust. One upgrade or one policy
decision can wipe out an entire source, while a new nonprofit
or a technical tweak can land me in a new world. I wish it
were less unstable, and I think that we should have more say.
Is it possible to be unaware of having a reading environment at
all? What would that be like, to just read?

THROW OUT THE TABLE

What follows are, in somewhat adapted form, three turns I took at a *Poetry International* online roundtable. Ilya Kaminsky moderated the roundtable, posing three questions to me and the Deaf poets Lilah Katcher and Karen Christie. I have removed Ilya's questions and cannot do Lilah and Karen justice by including their responses here.

I

What does it mean to be a DeafBlind poet today? First of all, being a DeafBlind poet means that, for my upcoming fortieth birthday, you should give me a gift card from Target, not Barnes and Noble. I have no use for a bookstore except for the Godiva chocolate bars they have. It's just that those bars are cheaper at Target.

It also means reading little contemporary poetry. This isn't the space to go into detail as to why not, but suffice it to say that no one responsible seems to care about Braille readers and poetry. My main source of poetry reading material is Project Gutenberg, a vast online database of books that are in the public domain. It's the best, easiest, most accessible. I urge you to donate money to support it, it's a vital resource.

I'm always startled when someone reads a poem of mine and says it reminds them of Frank O'Hara or Robert Lowell. I haven't read those poets; they haven't been dead for the required seventy years for their works to be released into the public domain. What I can see in that poem of mine is the hand of G. K. Chesterton, say, or Christina Rossetti.

It's strange, because to be a poet is a very DeafBlind thing. DeafBlind poets go back to at least the fifteenth century. True, true, there wasn't another one, not that I know of, until the eighteenth century. But a start is a start. The wonderful part is that we have such a rich literature. The tragic part is that distantism has something to do with the outpouring. A. F. Moritz once defined a poet as someone who turns isolation into solitude. We've always coped, and very well, too, with being locked out of much of society. Our books, letters, diaries, and knitted goods bear witness to that experience.

As usual, it's more complicated than that. Our community began to form in the second half of the nineteenth century when Morrison Heady and Laura Bridgman developed the practice of writing letters to any of us they could find. Distantism was too strong and our resources too limited for us to build a corporeal community, so the way to go was to create a virtual one. Sure, everyone back then wrote letters. Print culture reigned supreme. It wasn't just us who wrote letters; everyone did. But we made our correspondence network do more for us than writing did for anyone else. We invented online dating a long, long time ago. You wrote letters, you fell in love, and when the time was right, you went by stage then by rail to visit your beloved. A week later you proposed.

So it's not true that we write so much out of the marginalization we experience. It is a factor, and then there's the fact that writing is our home. Slowly, slowly, slowly, we constructed corporeal communities. Now we have the Protactile movement, the biggest, most dramatic claim we have ever made for the right to live as tactile people and to break down distantism. These developments are earthshaking. Yet our traditional virtual community, which made its transition to email very early in the Internet age, remains our primary space. Where you have people who literally write to exist, to socialize, and to perform many human functions, you bet there's poetry.

You have to understand. Virtually (exactly!) every significant DeafBlind historical figure was a poet. Morrison Heady published two collections. Laura Bridgman dabbled in it. Even Helen Keller couldn't resist knocking the canon on its head with "The Song of the Stone Wall." Richard Kinney, Robert J. Smithdas, Geraldine Lawhorn—poets all of them, in addition to the things they were more famous or tokenized for. Also, many, many don't realize that they have just written a poem. Some of them know it's poetry but don't care one whit about publishing.

You know the story that went viral, about a teenage girl "signing" with a DeafBlind man on a plane? Awful story, inspiration porn. But—it so happens the DeafBlind man, Tim Cook, is one of the greatest poets alive. [Tim Cook has since passed away.] I learned much about writing poetry from him just by hanging out with him when I spent some years on a listserv moderated by another great poet, the recently departed Melanie Ipo Kuu Bond. On that listserv, Tim was "De Jester," Melanie was "Momma Nature," and he gave me the nickname "Reverend Johnny" because I breathed fire in those days. I urged him to collect his wonderful poems into a book and have it published. He wasn't interested. He said that he wrote to delight his friends and that's all he wanted to do. Most of us write junk, fun junk, but trust me when I say that Tim Cook is different. And this hidden genius, who has flown on planes all his life, sometimes to meet someone he has fallen in love with, is suddenly party to a story that goes viral and the masses have no idea, and will never realize, just who he is. Why am I telling you all this? My main point is that a random DeafBlind person like that, it's no surprise he happens to be a poet.

II

Most abled people out there don't realize that there are many disability communities and further communities within each one. How do we navigate all those layers, overlapping and sometimes conflicting? Maybe it'd be good to talk about privilege and capital. There are competing privileges and sources of capital, which have currency in some spheres and none in others.

I was born as a basically sighted Deaf person, already half blind I'm sure, but I started life as what is called a Deaf of Deaf. My parents were Deaf, and this fact meant I had access to language at birth. Most Deaf and DeafBlind people don't have this privilege because they are born into hearing families, and there are additional problems when their parents freak out, feel guilt, call the cavalry to hammer everything they can into their poor babies' skulls. Often people say that I am lucky because I had Deaf parents. That's wrong, because everyone should have that. It should be the baseline, that you'd be born and your parents wouldn't freak out and you'd all communicate in a common language. Everyone should have that. Anything below that is deprivation.

But within the sighted Deaf world, it functions as a tremendous privilege. In that world, too, English is highly valued. Members of the elite speak ASL with a heavy English accent, fingerspelling many English words. Sometimes this is called the Gallaudet style, because Gallaudet alumni showed off their education in this way. There is a rift between the Gallaudet style and more authentic ASL. This was further complicated when ASL was recognized as a bona fide language and it became a hot commodity in the academy. I grew up picking up on two messages: English would be my meal ticket and ASL would be my meal ticket.

So it was already going to be a status booster if I ended up as an English poet, but as a child I showed no interest in reading. However, I was becoming increasingly blind and at one point I went into denial. This meant a period of isolation and it connected me with books, and every step in my changing vision led me to poetry. Meanwhile, I did grow up as something of an ASL adept, and I can imagine a trajectory where, had I never become blind, I'd still end up being an ASL poet.

It took me many years to figure it out, but ASL is not a DeafBlind language. My fluency in ASL necessarily eroded as I became a tactile person, and it was a personal loss. I mean, ASL is my first language. It's a big thing to lose one's first language, isn't it? With that loss went a great deal of my Deaf of Deaf capital and privileges.

This is hard to explain briefly, because there are so many things interwoven into it, but as much as ASL has been celebrated, English hegemony is overpowering. In our country the mainstream has often touted multiculturalism, but that always stops at multilingualism. For example, when I began to translate ASL poetry into English and looked for publications and grants, I found that it was assumed that foreign languages meant sources outside of the United States. There's a side of me that naturally wishes to resist this and to regard my own writings in English as automatically and deeply problematic. Often I have felt like I shouldn't write in English, because it meant doing some things that a portion of my community, due to various English literacy situations, won't be able to enjoy. In my family, we have removed as much of English as we can from our daily communication. Our decision saw a flowering of both ASL and Protactile.

Yet what is right or better for Deaf poets to do, what they need to be aware of if they choose to write in English, cannot be applied to DeafBlind poets. For one thing, we have no way to transmit Protactile over long distances. Sighted Deaf people now can make phone calls, send cellphone messages, and hold forth on social media all in ASL. That is wonderful and liberating. It poses a necessary threat to the universe. But we DeafBlind people must continue to use English, which remains the best way to communicate over long distances. We have our virtual spaces and traditions, we use flexible literacy approaches and often write in dialect and pidgin English. These facts make it less of a sin to be an English poet, but I still grapple with it. It is easier to be an English poet than to be a poet in a still-forbidden language like ASL, still harder to be a poet in an emerging language like Protactile. It is easier for English poets to be published and win grants. Writing in English reinforces English language dominance. Oh yes, it defiles and it corrupts. I assure you. So I proceed with qualms.

III

More and more academic and writing conferences are discussing inclusion and access. What are those topics' bearing on my life as a DeafBlind poet? I think that many of those conversations about access revolve around too narrow a basis. Maybe for many disability groups it is good because they gain full access when a few things are tinkered with. Also, the disability rights movement is bent on "integration" into mainstream society. If that's what they want, they should go for it and fight for it. But that drive toward integration often sweeps aside other perspectives and goals. A major difference is also that Deaf and DeafBlind people speak other languages, and mere access is almost never satisfactory.

Let me start with a simple example. I cannot tell you how many times someone asks me to check their organization's website and let them know if it's accessible. It's good that they want to make sure it is, but they're operating on a mistaken assumption. They assume that if the website is accessible, they are successfully including us. Not so. Websites are difficult to navigate via Braille. If you're sighted, you can see the whole screen at a glance and use the cursor to click on anything or touch the screen anywhere. Braille is different. It is one line of text at a time. For that reason, we love email and we hate to ever go online.

So the question should be how their organization can reach out to or include us, not how to make their website accessible. Do you see what I mean? The same misframing of the conversation happens over and over. In the scramble to include more people with disabilities in higher education, to use another example, universities may add to a job posting the words:

"People with disabilities are encouraged to apply." But they haven't asked the right questions yet. They've been unwittingly discriminatory every step of the way, and then they are puzzled. Why hasn't anyone with disabilities applied?

In this way, "inclusion" feels like a farce. These are invitations to fit in, not offers to include. And it's only the parts of us that can pass they'd like to have, not the whole of who we are or our worlds. It staggers me to see the word "diversity" thrown around so much these days, and perhaps it is true that there are new faces, that is important, but the format, the spaces, the schedule, the required qualifications, the evaluation systems, the length, the ways of doing things, the application forms, the submission processes, all of those things are the same. Exactly the same. Is diversity really happening?

Also, one DeafBlind person is not integration. Integration should mean more than one, the more the better. Integration should mean that the place is no longer a hearing-sighted place at all. If the place is still hearing-sighted, the format is hearing-sighted, hearing-sighted customs and ways of doing things prevail, inclusion is not happening. Technically, access may be there. Interpreters may be provided, captioning, whatever. All of those are superficial and often meaningless to me. Access as a means to include may work for some, but for me access is merely the by-product of true inclusion, for if a place changes, things are redesigned, many traditional accommodations will be rendered unnecessary. There are so many accommodations that seem necessary because what is attempted is fitting in.

Shouldn't we be asking different questions than questions of access? I know many, many Deaf poets, and there are many more DeafBlind poets. I know that we can benefit from the resources available in the poetry world. We can contribute. But they can't just say, "C'mon, apply!" They can't just say, "We'd like you to teach the summer workshop. Don't worry, we'll provide interpreters!" They need to ask different questions. "How do we get some of these grants into the hands of deserving DeafBlind poets?" They may find that they have to do it in a completely different way. They need to ask, "How would you like to teach poetry?" They may find that they need to throw out the big conference table in the middle of the room that they take so much for granted. I'm sorry, but so many of us are just not interested in fitting in. Indeed, we cannot. Instead, we're interested in collaboration. We're interested in changing the world.

ACKNOWLEDGMENTS

Taking their hands, I herd the following magazine editors to the parts of this book they will recognize. Excited pats and hugs go to:

Don Share, Lindsay Garbutt, and Holly Amos at *Harriet*: "Reading Environments"

Andrew Leland, Claire Boyle, and James Yeh at *McSweeney's*: "Against Access," "A Fable"

Nadja Spiegelman at *The Paris Review Daily*: "The View Where I Write"

Don Share, Lindsay Garbutt, and Holly Amos at *Poetry*: "Tactile Art"

Ilya Kaminsky at *Poetry International Online*: "Throw Out the Table"

Arthur Adler at *Scene4*: Part One of "No Stage"

Michael Northen at *Wordgathering*: "Distantism"

"Tactile Art," which won a National Magazine Award, also appeared in *The Best American Magazine Writing 2020*. Students in the University of Iowa Nonfiction Master of Fine Arts program chose "Against Access" for the Krause Essay Prize in 2022. Much of the book was written with indispensable financial support through a 2021–2023 Bush Leadership Fellowship and a 2020–2021 Disability Futures Fellowship.

One does not write alone. My fingers were entwined in the fingers of many others as I typed the words collected in *Touch the Future*. Especially present are the warm and probing thoughts of Sun Within (Jelica Nuccio), Fancy Cane (aj granda), Clamp and Shake (Halene Anderson), Skipping with Joy (Terra Edwards), Exacting (Cristina Hartmann), Two Assurances (Bryen Yunashko), The King with a Smile (Jaz Herbers), Curly Bear (Roberto Cabrera), Community Nudger (Hayley Broadway), Dorsal Effect (Robert Sirvage), Booksnake (Oscar Chacon), Ice Hop (Ahyicodae), Almost Too Cool (Lesley Silva-Kopec), 3arl (Earl Terry), Three Squeezes (CM Hall), Friendship Bracelet (Heather Holmes), Crasher (Soline Vennetier), Inclining Choreographies (Erin Manning), Toad (Brian Massumi), Growing Fern (Rhonda Voight-Campbell), Whorl (Victoria Magliocchino), Electrifying Happiness (Yashaira Romilus), Thinking Braces (Deanna Gagne), Neat Zipper (Mitch Holaly), Scampering in Pursuit of Study (Jessica Ennis), Giant Sweet Tooth (Jenny Lu), Gentle Beard (Gerard Williams), Fierce Beard (Raymond Luczak), Bumping Right Along (Donavan Williams), and Z (Vera Washington).

Many communities created the joy necessary to writing: The Protactile Network, the DeafBlind Studies group, the WritersCS group, the William James group, the Function of Reason group, the Poetics of Relation group, the schizz movements around 3 Ecologies and Tactile Communications, my fellow pilgrims, and the cohorts who stomped and danced through six DeafBlind Interpreting Institutes, the Protactile Language Interpreting Pilot Institute, and many Protactile Theory seminars.

The company of fellow writers during recent years shaped the book in another way. Deep admiration and appreciation out to Kaveh Akbar, Veronica Bickle, Katie Booth, Jim Cohn, Naomi Cohn, Gary Dop, Blair Fell, M. Leona Godin, Gabrielle Hodge, Paul Hostovsky, Rachel Kolb, Christopher Krentz, Aviya Kushner, Andrew Leland, Paige Lewis, Maren Linett, Aaron Pang, Carl Phillips, Ralph James Savarese, Robert Siebert, Kristin Snoddon, The Cyborg Jillian Weise, and James Yeh. For a formative education in the art of writing, I am indebted to the writers who gathered around various publications that my partner Adrean Clark and I edited between 1999 and 2011: Alison Aubrecht, the late Douglass Bullard, Karen Christie, Ryan Commerson, Willy Conley, Lindsay Dunn, the late Mervin D. Garretson, Kristen Harmon, Manny Hernandez, Christopher Jon Heuer, the late Judy Yaeger Jones, Aaron Weir Kelstone, the late Eric Malzkuhn, the late Nathie Marbury, the late Robert F. Panara, Curtis Robbins, Sara Stallard, Louise Stern, Scott Stoffel, Nick Sturley, Trudy Suggs, Mary Thornley, Michael Uniacke, the late Clayton Valli, Michele Westfall, the late Guy Wonder, Pamela Wright, and many others.

The following will never know how much they gave me during the time I was growing this book: Hallie Abelman, Xayan al-Amin, Nicole Alleman, Latif Ba, Ben Bahan, Carie Barrett-Lyon, H-Dirksen Bauman, Douglas C. Baynton, Ezra Benus, Sheila Black, Elisa Boettcher, Ryan Bondroff, Ed Borrone, Jill Bradbury, Tashi Bradford, Diane Brentari, Stephanie Burt, Corey Campbell, Deb and Brad Canaday, Aimee Chappelow, Shari Connelly, Wendy Darling, De Dudley, Catherine Durivage, Patti Durr, Dean Dykstra, Mary and Taras Dykstra, Cecilia Epps, Barry Esson, Julie Evans, Melissa Febos, Jim Ferris, Anita Forsberg, Jessica Friedman, Michele Friedner, Kenny Fries, Frank Gallimore, Meredith Gill, Jenna Gorlewicz, Mara Green, Kathryn Hale, Larissa Hanson, Wendy

Harris, Kelly Harrison, Mary Hartnett, Julie Hochgesang, Ashley Hoseth, Jada Johnson, Najma Johnson, Debra Kahn, Jennifer Keaton, Dorothy Kleeb, Chad and Anna Kramer, Harry Lang, Rubin Latz, Zihao Lin, Eric Lorberer, Paula Mac-Donald, Roderick Macdonald, Chris Martin, Dona Mathews, Laura Maudlin, Issy McGrath, Ben and Kelly McMaine, Mara Mills, Christine Mitchell, Lea Moynihan, Finn O'Dell, Ryan Ollis, Lois Pace, Greg and Barb Peck, Mitzi Peterson, Jenee Petri-Swanson, Christopher Phillips, Jeff Pollock, Erin Ramsay, Brent and Mavis Ransom, Richard Raschke, Gloria and the late beloved Randall Reese, Lois Remmers, Elio Riggillo, Nancy Riley, Kris Ringman, Octavian Robinson, Mick Ross, Rocky Rothschild, Rebecca Sanchez, Doug and Jill Schober, Luke and Lindsey Schraw, Jon Skaalen, Danez Smith, Theresa B. Smith, Shari Stamps, Elizabeth Steyer, Marian and Erwin Stobbe, Tan Siew Ling, Ron Thomke, Nicole Thornberg, Lisa van der Mark, Anna and Harold Van Sickle, Inara Verzemnieks, Bruce Visser, Mary Weed, Morgan Grayce Willow, Kathi Wolfe, and a host of others.

This book wouldn't have found its way into your hands without the loving advocacy of my first agent, Tina Pohlman. When she assumed the executive editorship of a publishing house, Sally Wofford-Girand generously took me on. Thank you.

For their intense care and attention to detail, I am grateful to my editors at W. W. Norton & Company, Jill Bialosky and Drew Weitman. My thanks to the copyeditor, Janet McDonald, and to the cover designers and interior designers, publicists and marketers who believed in *Touch the Future*.

The shades of dearly departed mentors, friends, and kin continue to bring calm and joy: Harry C. Anderson, Jeff Bohrman, Melanie Bond, Tricia Borman, Tim Cook, Betty

Dooley, Denise Dooley, Jerry Dooley, Cathy Erickson, Paul and Nelle Halverson, Esther Hathaway, Paul Koster, Geraldine Lawhorn, Stephen Medlicott, Kathy and Gerry Meyers, Isaac Obie, Leslie Paul Peterson, my grandparents Alvin and Hazel Wahlin, and my uncle Kenny Wahlin.

To Mom and Dad; to my siblings, Keith, Paula, and Diego; to Aunt Esther; and to Jane and Stan: Thank you for being there and sharing in my many excitements.

Breathing through every page of my small offering is the life in a home made new every day by my best friend and partner Adrean, our Jael, our Armand, our Azel, our Angel, and our Nibby. My heart on your heart.

ALSO AVAILABLE FROM
JOHN LEE CLARK:

Finalist for the National Book Award for Poetry
Finalist for the Kingsley Tufts Poetry Award
Winner of the Minnesota Book Award for Poetry

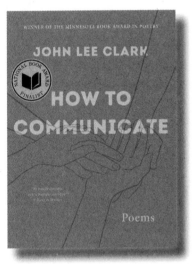

"[John Lee] Clark's writing is full of humor and life."
—Andrew Leland, *The New Yorker Radio Hour*

"*How to Communicate* is a masterpiece."   —Kaveh Akbar,
New York Times best-selling author of *Martyr!*

"As tonally dynamic as it is formally inventive."
—*Poets & Writers*

W. W. NORTON & COMPANY
Independent Publishers Since 1923